CRIME-PROOF

CRIME-PROOF

Protecting Yourself, Your Family and Your Property

Edited by Marilyn A. Moore
with Sally Deneen

Managing Editor: Elizabeth Grudzinski

KNIGHT-RIDDER, INC.

ANDREWS AND McMEEL
A Universal Press Syndicate Company
Kansas City

Additional copies of this book may be ordered by calling
(800) 642-6480.

Library of Congress Cataloging–in–Publication Data

Crime-Proof / Knight-Ridder Corporation.
   p.   c.m
 ISBN 0-8362-8079-2 (generic) : $6.95
 1. Crime prevention—United States—handbooks, manuals, etc.
I. Knight-Ridder (Firm)
HV7431.C775 1994
362.88—dc20   94-3700
                                                    CIP

Contents

Acknowledgments

Crime-Proof was compiled from reports and graphics supplied by the following Knight-Ridder Inc. companies:

Akron Beacon-Journal
The Charlotte Observer
Detroit Free Press
(Gary) *Post-Tribune*
Knight-Ridder Tribune Information Services
(Long Beach) *Press-Telegram*
The Miami Herald
The Philadelphia Daily News

Special thanks to:

Terry Sheridan for assistance with Chapter 1
Bob Portenier for assistance with Chapter 3
Alliance for Fraud in Telemarketing
American Bankers Association
American Hotel and Motel Association
The Associated Press
Bank Administration Institute
Better Business Bureau Philanthropic Advisory
Call for Action, Inc.
Child Find of America
Federal Trade Commission
The *Miami Herald* editorial art department
National Burglar and Fire Alarm Association

National Charities Information Bureau
National Consumer Fraud Task Force
National Crime Prevention Council
National Crime Prevention Institute
National Foundation for Consumer Credit
National Insurance Crime Bureau
National Safety Council
National Sheriff's Association
National Victim Center
Police departments across the country
Security on Campus, Inc.

Introduction

Crime Prevention Begins with Us

Far from the marble corridors of justice, far from the chambers of lawmakers where the debate over crime continues, citizens across the United States are taking a fresh approach to crime fighting.

Their goal: to become crime-proof.

They are educating themselves, learning protective techniques and skills that will help reduce their chances of becoming crime victims. Far from feeling helpless, they believe they play an important role in avoiding crime. It's not totally in their hands, but they know there are steps to cut their chances of becoming a statistic . . . and they're taking them.

That means they know the answers to the following questions and are doing something about them:

1. It's late at night. Everyone's asleep. Suddenly, you hear glass breaking. A burglar is inside the house. What do you do?

2. You're on a tight budget and you haven't used your credit cards for two months. They're locked up in a drawer

at home. One day, $2,000 in strange charges appear on a charge card bill in your name. How could that have happened?

3. A purse snatcher grabs an elderly woman's purse. Should she hold onto the purse strap? Should she sit down on the sidewalk? Should she throw her purse at the crook?

4. You're stopped on a deserted expressway ramp. A shadow materializes in your driver's side mirror. It's a menacing-looking man approaching your car from behind. Should you run the red light?

5. Your child is walking down the street with a friend. A car pulls up beside them. The driver asks for directions. What should your youngster do?

The answers are in this book.

Compiled from reports that have appeared in Knight-Ridder newspapers nationwide and from other reliable sources, this book stresses commonsense tips that can make a difference.

Each chapter addresses a specific concern: crime-proofing your home, yourself, your children, your car and your money. Other chapters focus on the special issues that affect women, the elderly, college students, travelers and others.

Read the book quickly for information that is useful to you today. Use it as an encyclopedia, referring to those pages that will be relevant as needs arise. Because the book is organized as a reference, some repetition of basic safety information is deliberate. Cross-references refer to fuller discussion of a particular issue. The statistics are the latest available.

Just about anything you need to know about basic crime prevention is here. Many crimes occur because someone forgot or disregarded common sense. Other crimes demand

How often are crimes committed in the U.S.?

Every two seconds a serious crime is committed in this country.

Other statistics:

One property crime every . . .	**3 seconds**
One larceny-theft every . . .	**4 seconds**
One burglary every . . .	**11 seconds**
One motor vehicle theft every . . .	**20 seconds**
One violent crime every . . .	**22 seconds**
One aggravated assault every . . .	**28 seconds**
One robbery every . . .	**47 seconds**
One forcible rape every . . .	**5 minutes**
One murder every . . .	**22 minutes**

Larceny-theft is the most commonly committed crime

Types of serious crimes committed in the U.S., as percent of total, 1992:

Larceny-theft	**54.8%**
Burglary	**20.6%**
Motor vehicle theft	**11.1%**
Aggravated assault	**7.8%**
Robbery	**4.7%**
Forcible rape	**0.8%**
Murder	**0.2%**

SOURCE: Federal Bureau of Investigation 1992 Uniform Crime Reports

a pro-active approach, requiring you to exercise judgment according to the situation and your personal comfort level.

The first step in crime-proofing is deciding to take an active stance against crime. Educate yourself. Be prepared to act—and react—in ways that cut your odds of becoming a victim and being hurt physically, emotionally and financially.

"The whole basis for crime prevention is trying to get people to be responsible on their own," says Janet Kinsella, a police spokeswoman in Palm Beach County, Fla. "The thing people can do to prevent crime is to remove the opportunity."

The key word is opportunity. Don't offer a criminal that chance. That's what crime-proofing is about—keeping the odds on your side.

For More Information:

The National Crime Prevention Council, 1700 K Street NW, Second Floor, Washington, D.C. 20006-3817. 202-466-6272.

The National Safety Council, 1121 Spring Lake Drive, Itasca, IL 60143. 1-800-621-7619.

National Sheriffs' Association, 1450 Duke St., Alexandria, VA 22314. 1-800-424-7827.

National Victim Center, 309 W. Seventh St., Suite 705, Fort Worth, TX 76102. 1-800-FYI-CALL.

---

1 🏠

Crime-Proofing
Your Home

It's a long-heard lament: Police can't cope. The courts are jammed. Prisons are stuffed. Everyone demands solutions.

Congress argues over tougher sentences, boot camps, gun control, drug clinics and more police. No one seems certain what will really clamp down on crime. Should the cure come from increases in social workers, money for inner cities or funding for schools? Should we build more prisons and more courthouses? The one thing that's clear in this murky debate is that while the policymakers struggle for consensus, criminals are still committing crimes.

Is there anything you can do?

Meet Christopher Reed, 28, a bus driver from Miami. He's never been a victim of crime, perhaps because he's so prepared. His home has a burglar alarm. It has good deadbolt locks, a fence and spotlights that come on at dusk.

People like Reed don't put their lives on hold. They've become "hard targets," people who don't give criminals the opportunity to commit crime. You can do it, too.

Begin with your home. Most homeowners and tenants ignore common sense when it comes to home security, police say. And burglars would like you to keep it that way.

Nighttime is when many of us think about burglars and ways to thwart them. But experienced thieves prefer to work in daylight, when a home is most likely to be empty. "A burglar looks for visual clues that a home is unoccupied," says Joe Mele, assistant professor at the National Crime Prevention Institute in Louisville, Ky. A morning newspaper on the porch, mail spilling from the mailbox, an open garage are all ways of saying, "Rob me."

What can you do to send a different message?

"Go out to the curb and survey your house," advises Helen Maxwell, who became a crime prevention expert after a home invasion. "Go to the back alley and do the same thing. Do that in the daytime, do that at night."

Ask yourself: How fast can someone get into the house? Can an intruder slip in without making much noise? How would I get in if I lost my keys? Can the entrances to the house be seen from the street? Does a wall, wooden fence or shrubbery create a hiding place for an intruder? Is there access to the roof or an upper-story window from a nearby wall, drain pipe or tree? Can a wall-unit air conditioner be removed from outside?

Many police departments offer a crime prevention survey of your home. They can help tell you where the weak spots are in your security web.

For example, Detective Travis Ogle of the Metro-Dade Police Department in Miami sees lots of homeowners who ignore crime prevention advice regarding landscaping. "The vegetation should be no higher than the knee," he says. "If you have trees, get them so that they have canopies that do not drop below 10 feet." But some people won't give up garden aesthetics for security.

The result of this kind of inaction: burglaries. In 1992, nearly three million properties were burglarized—or 21 percent of all the crimes that are counted by FBI statistics. The region with the highest burglary volume was the South, with 41 percent of the total. Western states experienced 24 percent of the nation's burglaries, the Midwest 20 percent, and the Northeast 16 percent. The good news: Unlike some other crimes, burglary rates are trending downward, down 7 percent from 1988 and 5 percent from 1983.

When are housebreakers hardest at work? In August, according to FBI statistics. February is the slowest month.

Police will tell you that most burglars are young—in their teens and early 20s—male amateurs looking for a quick heist.

Favorite targets are the homes of working couples who often spend more on stereos, CD players, computers, VCRs, TVs and other electronics that burglars prize. Best of all, from a burglar's point of view, working couples are usually gone all day.

Your goal, then, is twofold: Make burglars pass by your house because it looks too tough to break into, or if they do try to enter, present enough obstacles to make them give up.

Basic Home Security Tips

The following practical tips will help secure your property right now. They require little or no financial investment—instead, they demand only a strong measure of common sense:

❑ Lock doors and windows, including skylights. Intruders look for the easiest entry. Also, burglars know that forcible entry to a home carries a more severe criminal

Types of housing

Your common sense, coupled with basic security measures, can help make your home less appealing to burglars. Remember, too, that many police departments have crime prevention officers who will do a security check of your home and suggest improvements. The following, while not intended to be comprehensive, is a start in your considerations.

There are no hard-and-fast rules about what type of home is more secure than another. Indeed, sociological studies have indicated that if residents fail to combine their physical and social environments, they increase the risk of crime, said Jean

Apartments/condos

■ **Fewer points** of entry.

■ **Neighbors**, by sheer closeness alone, are more apt to know if something's amiss. On the other hand, they may assume someone else will report a problem.

■ **Certain common** areas — laundry and storage rooms — will need more surveillance.

■ **Is a building manager** on site? What hours?

■ **Is there** a gated main entry? Intercom at the building door?

■ **Check** if you are allowed to reinforce or change locks on windows and doors. In condos, for example, association rules may not allow certain items or changes.

■ **High-rise units** may not be safer than low-rise: buildings can be scaled by climbers.

Townhomes

■ **Courtyards** can promote privacy, but those that are entirely enclosed make it easy for intruders to work unobserved from the outside.

■ **Owners** have more control over front and back yards. But common areas between and around buildings may make neighbors less likely to question someone walking around the property.

■ **More entry points**: garage, sliding glass doors, front doors, windows.

SOURCE: Herald research

O'Neil, director of research and policy analysis for the National Crime Prevention Council in Washington, D.C. In other words, how neighbors interact with each other makes a difference.

General considerations, beyond personal income and lifestyle preferences, include: Will you live alone? Are you a single parent? What age are your children? Does your spouse travel frequently? Is the community still under construction? How frequent are police patrols? How long is police response time to your home? Is there limited traffic access?

But here are specific housing style considerations.

Single-family

■ **More** entry points.

■ **More** likely to have shrubs or trees that could provide hiding places or access.

■ **Space** is clearly defined, and neighbors likely will know who belongs on a property.

■ **Increased sense** of "mental investment" in the neighborhood.

■ **The lower density** of the neighborhood may mean more interaction among neighbors but also means fewer people are around to observe anything suspicious.

Gated communities

■ **Guards, gates and fences** create psychological barriers. Police refer to it as the expectation of privacy.

■ **On the other hand**, fences can also afford privacy to the burglar. And gates break down.

HIRAM HENRIQUEZ, PHILL FLANDERS and REGINALD MYERS / The Herald

penalty than trespassing through an unlocked door.

❑ Don't leave garage doors open. Also, lock doors leading into the house from the garage.

❑ Don't hide extra home keys outside, the experts say. If you must, pick a clever spot. Avoid the obvious: under the mat or in the mailbox.

❑ Make sure your mailbox is large enough to hold its contents and that it closes securely. Burglars look for mailboxes brimming with letters as a sign no one is home. Don't put your name on the mailbox.

❑ At night, keep lights on in more than one room.

❑ Consider getting a dog. It need not be a Great Dane. The idea is to create noise, which wards off burglars. Keep in mind that while the barking is a deterrent, burglars can disable animals by dousing them with tear gas or clubbing them. (See more information about owning dogs for security purposes in Chapter 7.)

❑ If a stranger comes to the door asking to use the phone, don't let him or her inside. Offer to place the call.

❑ Be aware that some thieves pose as repair people, meter readers or utility workers. Request identification if you feel uneasy or suspicious. Call the main office to verify their credentials.

❑ Consider getting a cellular phone. Put it in the bedroom so you can dial for help. "A lot of home intruders will either cut the phone lines or they will shut down the power, which will nullify an alarm system if it doesn't have a battery backup," Helen Maxwell says.

❑ Engrave your driver's license number on valuables so they can be identified if lost or stolen. Record the serial numbers, model numbers and value of those items, and videotape or photograph them as an inventory. Keep the information in a safe-deposit box or other safe place. Check with your local police department to see whether you can borrow an engraving tool.

❏ If you hide valuables, put them in places burglars won't think to look. For instance, burglars know that people hide jewelry in the kitchen, in toilet tanks and in dresser drawers. So where do police advise you to hide your things? "We don't suggest places," says Officer D.A. Winchester of the Charlotte, N.C., police. "Burglars also read."

❏ Keep a map of your hiding places and store it in a safe-deposit box or with a trusted friend.

❏ When a new stereo, TV or home computer arrives, don't put the labeled carton in the trash unless you flatten it and turn it inside out.

❏ During holidays, keep packages and gift boxes away from windows so that burglars won't be tempted to break in.

❏ Form a Neighborhood Watch group. Most police departments will help residents start one. In turn, look around the neighborhood for things that could contribute to crime:

For more information, contact:

Jean O'Neil of the National Crime Prevention Council suggests the following sources for more information on securing your home:

☛ Contact your local police department's crime prevention officer. Ask for a free security survey of your home.

☛ Check your public library for free public information bulletins.

☛ Write the National Crime Prevention Council, 1700 K Street NW, Second Floor, Washington, D.C. 20006-3817. Ask for the F1 packet, which contains information on general crime prevention and residential security.

How to safeguard your home

Some tips for crime-proofing your home:

Deadbolts are best

Deadbolt locks with a minimum one-inch throw cannot be jimmied open easily.

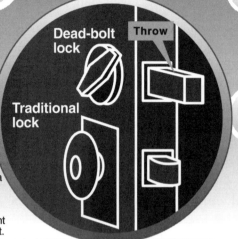

Dead-bolt lock

Throw

Traditional lock

Exterior doors

- Use solid, 1 3/4 inch metal or hardwood doors.
- Use good locks on all doors, including those to garages and sheds.
- Secure sliding glass doors with bars, locks or a wooden dowel placed in the door track; a screw partially seated in the overhead track will prevent doors from being lifted out.

Windows
- Use good locks

Porches, outside areas
- Should be well-lighted

Extra keys
- Should be entrusted to a neighbor, not hidden under a doormat.

Yard
- Trim bushes and trees so they do not hide doors or windows; keep ladders and yard tools inside.

Alarm systems
- Summon help in an emergency; your local law enforcement agency can assess your needs.

SOURCES: National Crime Prevention Council, Bureau of Justice Statistics; research by PAT CARR

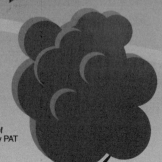

poor street lighting, abandoned cars, vacant lots, littered playgrounds with broken equipment, or homes that elderly or impoverished owners have trouble maintaining.

Building Blocks to Home Security

Regardless of the type of home you live in, you can take many steps to make it more secure.

Use the practical precautions outlined at the beginning of this chapter as a building block to more technical, mechanical considerations described below. Features such as lighting, landscaping, windows and doors can do much to discourage would-be burglars.

Lighting. Lighting can be among your most powerful weapons in keeping your home safe. Criminals love the dark because it hides their handiwork.

Illuminate all possible entry points, including areas under windows. If the space around a window or door is dark, a burglar will feel more at ease taking the time necessary to force it open. Be careful with floodlights that unwittingly create shadowed places for people to hide.

Crime prevention experts recommend two types of exterior lighting: photo-sensitive systems that come on automatically as natural light diminishes, and motion-triggered lights. Motion-sensor lights should be installed at vulnerable locations, such as over entryways, garage doors and accessible windows. Exterior lights should be connected to timers that automatically turn them on at dusk and off in the morning.

Outdoor lights should be made of unbreakable plastic or covered with wire mesh to prevent thieves from smashing out bulbs.

Inside your home, use timers that switch lights on and off

Lighting

■ **Illuminate all entries.** If the space around a window or door is dark, a burglar will feel more at ease taking the time necessary to open it.

■ **Exterior.** Crime prevention officials recommend two types: photo-sensitive systems that operate automatically as natural light diminishes, and motion-triggered lights.

■ **Interior.** Use timers that switch lights on and off at preset times. But vary the pattern. Lights that click on and off at the same time every day tell a burglar checking on your home for several nights that you're away. Ask a neighbor to reset the timers every few days.

■ **Keep clean and well lighted:** Entrances, parking areas, hallways, stairways, laundry rooms, mailboxes.

SOURCES: National Crime Prevention Council, Bureau of Justice Statistics, Alpine Electric Co.; research by PAT CARR

Knight-Ridder Tribune/PAUL TRAP and PAT CARR

at preset times. But vary the pattern. Lights that click on and off at the same time every day tell a burglar checking on your home for several nights that you're away. Ask a neighbor to reset the timers every few days.

Landscaping. Don't let shrubbery and trees obscure entrances and provide hiding places. Keep shrubs trimmed below window level. Also, trim them at the bottom so the feet and legs of an intruder can be seen easily. Think: Where would you hide if you were a home intruder?

Prune tree branches and remove trellises if they provide access to second-floor windows. Plant thorny bushes around windows to discourage burglars.

Windows. The tougher you make openings to break through, the more likely a prospective burglar will move on to a less well-defended home.

Make sure you have extra locks to secure window panels together or prevent them from being lifted out of the frame or track. Install locks on skylights, too.

Consider having shatter-resistant safety film applied to window glass.

Air-conditioning units or fans in a window opening should be bolted in place. Wrought-iron security cages can be installed around them.

If you know certain windows won't be opened for ventilation, seal them shut permanently.

Doors. Get solid wood or steel exterior doors. They should fit securely in the jamb. If doors have glass panels or are near a window, deadbolts should be double cylinder, which requires a key both indoors and outdoors. Store the key away from the door, but put it in a safe place so it can be easily reached in an emergency.

Have peepholes with a 180-degree view in every entry door.

Front doors should be easily visible from the street. Police patrolling your neighborhood cannot see what's happening on your front stoop if the front door opens sideways into the house. "Some people have a side entry door," says Leo Bellon, a Miami architect. "This is easy for a burglar. Nobody can see them from the street so they can spend a lot of time opening your door."

Doors with hinges exposed on the outside should have pins or nails placed in the doorjamb. That way a burglar can't pull out the hinges and remove the door.

Sliding patio doors should lock from the inside. For extra protection, place a strip of wood or metal in the lower track. Put protruding flat-head screws in the upper track to prevent burglars from taking off the doors.

For French doors, consider getting a jimmy-resistant vertical deadbolt. If mounted correctly, it pins the two doors together.

Door frames should be strong, with few gaps between them and the door. Otherwise, burglars can use prying tools to force their way into the home.

All doors should be sturdy. If burglars get no answer at the front door, they often go around to the back or side doors, which are often flimsy and in locations that offer them privacy from neighbors' eyes. An experienced thief can use a pry bar, wrench or shovel to force a door open in seconds and be out in three to five minutes with the loot.

Don't forget your overhead garage door: Keep it locked.

When away from home, manually lock the garage door—put a sturdy padlock in the ceiling track, for example. Don't rely on your automatic door opener as a locking mechanism. An electronic garage door opener should be of the multi-frequency variety so the door cannot be accidentally opened by the sound of an airplane overhead.

Windows and doors

Burglars look for unlocked or open windows and doors, or those easily pried open.

The tougher you make openings to break through, the more likely a prospective burglar will move on.

Windows

- **Have extra locks** to secure panels together or prevent them from being lifted out of the frame or track.
- **Secure glass panels** with break-resistant plastic.
- **Air-conditioning units** or fans in a window opening should be bolted in place.
- **If you know** certain windows won't be opened for ventilation, seal them.
- **Skylights** require locks.

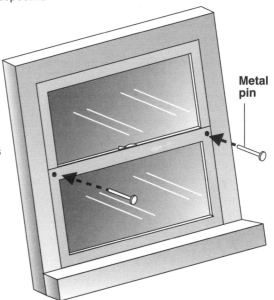

Metal pin

Doors

- **Sliding patio doors** should lock from the inside. Place a strip of wood or metal in the lower track and seat a protruding flat-head screw in the upper track.
- **Use solid wood** or steel exterior doors.
- **Keep garage doors**, and interior doors leading from the garage into the house, locked. When away, manually lock the garage door – put a padlock in the track, for example. Don't rely on your automatic door opener as a locking mechanism.
- **Door frames** should be strong, with few gaps between them and the door.
- **Side and back doors** should be as sturdy as front doors.

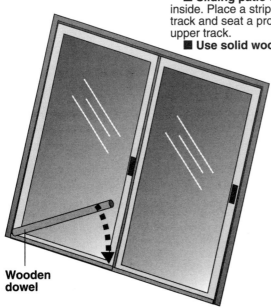

Wooden dowel

Consider the interior door connecting to the garage as an entry door, even though it isn't exposed to the outdoors. It should be solid core, not hollow.

Locks. Buy the best locks you can afford, and use them. "A lot of people use rinky-dink hardware and the burglar is in and out," says Joe Mele of the National Crime Prevention Institute.

But the best locking hardware in the world won't do much good on a flimsy door and frame. Be sure your door is solid and that the frame is sturdy.

Replace or rekey all locks before you move in.

The National Crime Prevention Institute recommends that all entry doors be equipped with deadbolt locks. Don't use push-button or turn-tab locks.

Deadbolt locks are not a replacement for alarm systems. "We recommend formidable locks and hardware, backed up with an alarm," says Mele. This requires burglars to waste precious time trying to force open the door, triggering the alarm while they're still outside.

Security bars. Security bars keep burglars out very well, but they also keep homeowners trapped inside in a fire. "Fire-wise, there is no good burglar bar," says Robert Pudney, fire chief in Plantation, Fla.

Because of fire safety concerns, some cities permit security bars; some don't. Check with your local police department or municipal building and zoning department about installing security bars.

Even built-in safety escape mechanisms aren't foolproof. For example, security bars with key locks can be a problem if no one can find the keys in a smoky interior.

Pin-released security guards, which many fire officials approve, work like this: The guards are attached to the exterior wall of the house with 12-inch iron pins that run

How a Deadbolt Works

A deadbolt lock usually is drilled above the knob and equipped with a steel shaft that moves into a strikeplate on the doorjamb when the key is turned. That shaft should be no less than an inch long and preferably 1 1/2 inches. A shallower shaft may not penetrate deeply enough into the doorjamb to stay secure if the door is kicked.

The strikeplate, which is cut into the doorjamb, also should be secured with screws that are not easily dislodged, usually 2 1/2 inches long. Lock manufacturers sometimes provide screws as short as 3/4 inch, Mele says, but these are often not long enough for best security. The 2 1/2 -inch wood screws fasten deep into the timbers around the door, keeping the strikeplate secure.

Another tip: If the deadbolt's cylinder juts out from the door's exterior, it should be mounted within a solid, round piece of steel with sides that slope at a 45-degree angle. These sloping sides make it nearly impossible for thieves to grip and twist off the cylinder with a wrench.

---

through the wall and into the house. On the inside, the pin is secured by a T-shaped cotter pin.

In case of a fire, the cotter pin is pulled free, the long pins are pushed out through the wall, and the entire window guard swings open, freeing the window for escape. The guard can be reinstalled by pushing the pins back into the walls and securing the cotter pin.

Safes. A home safe can provide a secure repository for valuables and important papers, if you choose the appropriate kind.

Safes come in many sizes and offer various degrees of protection from fire or burglary. Some larger, more expensive ones safeguard against both. Consider the value of the items the safe will contain, and how much you're willing to spend for the safe.

Assess your needs first. Gather your valuables into a pile and then buy a safe that's 25 percent larger than the pile, advises Kelly Sadar, owner of Kelly's Southport Lock & Safe in Fort Lauderdale. That way the safe will accommodate your future needs.

Ask your insurance company whether you'll get a discount on your premiums if you buy a safe that's highly rated. A B-rated safe door is a basic burglary safe with two relocking devices. A C-rated safe door has a thicker, heavier door with hardplate reinforcement. "The higher the rating, the harder it is to get in," Sadar says.

If you are concerned about valuables during your absence, you'll likely need a safe that weighs several hundred pounds. It will have to be anchored to the floor so it can't be taken away and opened later.

A fireproof safe will not offer burglary protection. Why? "Fire containers are just what they are—they are for protecting paper from a fire," Sadar says. A fireproof unit has thick doors and walls of light-gauge steel, but a burglar can open it in no time with a crowbar.

Burglary-resistant safes generally are constructed of high-density steel, concrete or high-density alloys. Key-guarded safes are not usually strong enough. Get a dial-guarded safe, instead. If you can't remember combinations, get a new digital safe. They have round dials with 10 numbers, and you decide which number will be your combination—Social Security number, for example. Don't use your phone number, address or something obvious that a burglar may try.

Don't store important papers or rarely used valuables in a home safe. Use a safe-deposit box at a bank or other high-security facility.

Alarm Systems

Home alarm systems are effective at detecting and thwarting intruders and come in a wide range of service, function and expense. Basically, they include a central control box, activation/deactivation device or control, varying types of sensors and a siren.

How much assurance the system will afford you depends a great deal on how thorough a shopper you have been. "You have to assess your particular situation, with pets, kids, seniors and the complexity of turning something on and off," says Long Beach, Calif., police spokeswoman Karen Kerr.

Be sure to compare features, monitoring and maintenance agreements. *Consumer Reports* rates both dealer-installed and do-it-yourself systems; back issues are available at your local library. The National Burglar and Fire Alarm Association offers a brochure called, "Considerations When Looking for a Home Burglar Alarm System." Call 301-907-3202.

Here's what to assess before you begin your search:

❏ **Your needs.** Figure out what you want to protect: the perimeter of the house (yard, doors, windows) and/or interior. What valuables do you have and where do you keep them? How many people will have access to the alarm code and controls? How old are your children? Do you have pets? Do people come and go at set times, or haphazardly? Do you have babysitters, a cleaning service or other regular visitors? Do you want just intruder detection, or also fire, smoke or medical alerts? Do you want the system monitored by an outside service?

❏ **Your budget.** Costs vary from several hundred dollars for do-it-yourself installations to well into the thousands for professionally installed systems. "A burglar alarm gives a homeowner peace of mind, and you can't put a price tag on peace of mind," says Linda Gimbel, of the National Burglar and Fire Alarm Association in Bethesda, Md.

❏ **Types of systems.** Alarms are wired or wireless.

Wired alarms operate through sensors linked by wires to a central control unit. It is armed and disarmed at a wall-mounted control pad; the central control unit is a wall-mounted box typically hung in a closet or out-of-the-way spot. Because of that, it is more difficult to disable than a wireless system. Wired systems generally include more features, such as outside monitoring, panic buttons, and fire/smoke/medical alerts. The house can be zoned, and armed individually.

With a wireless system, a transmitter communicates with the central control. The alarm can be activated and deactivated through a remote control; zoned activation also is possible. The control box typically contains the siren, which can be disabled by an intruder.

Alarm systems can offer three types of defense—perimeter, area and object protection:

❏ **Perimeter sensors** protect the entrances to your house—doors, windows, skylights. For example, magnet-operated sensors can tell you if a door or window is opened. Glass breakage detectors sense sounds or shock waves from breaking glass. Alarm screens can detect a cut or break in window screens.

❏ **Area protection devices** often guard interiors; they are an invisible means of protection in a high-risk area. Examples include ultrasound and microwave devices that detect motion, or infrared sensors that detect changes in heat.

❏ **Object protection** can include "traps" on jewelry boxes, drawers and safes.

How to Shop for an Alarm System

Some police departments prefer alarm systems that are monitored by security companies. "It's like someone watching your house," says Patrick Brickman, a detective for Metro-Dade Police in Miami.

Here's how it works: An activated alarm signal travels over phone lines to a central station. Operators there will call your home. If there is no answer, or the phone is busy, or whoever answers is unable to provide the security code word or number, police will be summoned to your home.

"It's more than equipment—it's a service," adds Mark Legot, of Burglar Alarm Technicians, a Fort Lauderdale security company.

However, false alarms are a major concern. Neighbors find them irritating; police see them as a waste of effort. Every time your alarm accidentally trips, it increases indifference to the alarm. Police say burglars who stake out neighborhoods know which houses are prone to false alarms.

Police departments increasingly fine homeowners after a certain number of "free" false alarms. In Long Beach, Calif., for example, the fine is $300 after the fifth false alarm.

Ask your local police department whether you need an alarm permit. Be aware that failing to register the alarm with the police could mean a fine. If you fail to pay up, police may not respond to alarms at your home.

Here are some questions to ask about alarm monitoring services:

❏ What is the monitoring agreement's cost and duration?

❏ Do you have to have the monitoring service if you lease or buy the system? Some companies won't lease the system unless you have monitoring.

❏ In a power failure, what is the station's backup power?

❏ What happens if telephone lines are cut? Most alarm systems operate on phone lines to dial the monitoring service. Special devices can detect whether a line has been cut and alert authorities.

❏ Is the monitoring station operated 24 hours, 365 days a year?

❏ Is there a service contract available?

When considering an alarm company, friends and neighbors are a good reference source. Be sure to ask them if they would get the same type of alarm again.

Question warranties and agreements. Whose "lifetime" does a lifetime warranty cover?

Contracts vary and warrant a close reading. Review carefully a claim of free installation. That sometimes comes with a monitoring agreement only.

Check the alarm company's credentials with state and local officials. If alarm contractors can have several types of licenses in your state, find out what the differences are. Does the state have an electrical contractor licensing board that governs alarm contractors? If so, have any complaints been filed with that board against the company?

Does your state require that companies do background checks on their employees? If not, does the company have that policy anyway? Does the company use subcontractors? If so, are their employees subject to background checks?

Is the company listed with Underwriters Laboratories? UL-listed companies face annual inspections and must meet guidelines for performance and equipment.

For information about burglar alarms, contact the National Burglar and Fire Alarm Association, 7101 Wisconsin Ave., Suite 901, Bethesda, Md. 20814. Or call 301-907-3202. This association will send you a list of member companies in your area and will tell you whether they have appropriate state licenses.

An Intruder Within

You've maintained the exterior of your house, trimmed the landscaping, invested in doors, locks and alarm systems. And you know about checking identification of workers and keeping doors locked, and so on.

Still, it happens. You suspect an intruder is inside your home. What to do?

If you arrive home to find the door ajar, do not enter. The burglar may still be inside, and a confronted burglar can be dangerous. Instead, call the police from a neighbor's house or pay phone.

If you awaken to find an intruder in your bedroom, crime prevention expert Joe Mele says you should pretend to be asleep.

If someone enters the house while family members are awake and about, the general advice is: run. Try to escape.

Your individual ability to adapt to a crisis is key to surviving a home invasion or even the accidental interruption of a robbery.

The plan has to be yours to devise, one you and your family are comfortable with and can carry out.

You may consider guiding everyone into a so-called safe room, equipped with a cellular phone and perhaps reinforced with concrete or plywood that could allow it to serve double-duty as a storm shelter. Or plan to shepherd everyone out a back door or window, into a neighbor's yard.

The message here—from keeping your name off the mailbox to elaborate alarm systems—is to have a plan. Or as

Helen Maxwell, the woman robbed in her Missouri home, put it: live defensively. After all, it's only common sense.

Going On Vacation

A vacation for you isn't a vacation for a burglar. The moment you leave, a thief could decide it's time to go to work. What's the best way to prepare your house?

"When you go on vacation, you are basically abandoning your property," says Fort Lauderdale Police Sgt. Robert Smith. "If someone knows they have time in a house, they usually do a pretty good job going through it."

Here are precautions you can take to reduce that risk.

❏ Stop mail and newspaper deliveries. Or get someone to pick them up daily. Sometimes a change in routine—such as having no newspapers lying on the lawn for even a few minutes a day—can tip off a burglar scouting the neighborhood.

❏ Tell police you're going on vacation and that you would like them to keep an eye on the house. Let them know if a neighbor has permission to go inside the house to check on things. Consider writing a permission letter and leaving it with the neighbor to head off any confusion.

❏ Ask neighbors to remove pizza coupons or anything else that solicitors hang on your front doorknob. Arrange for routine maintenance, such as having snow shoveled, the grass mowed or the garbage put out on pickup days. It's also good if someone you trust enters the house occasionally to raise or lower the shades and pull curtains in various rooms.

❏ Put lights and a radio or television on timers. Put two or more lights on a timer year-round (not just when you're away) to make it harder for casing burglars to judge when you're gone.

❏ Don't pull down shades and blinds if you don't nor-

How to protect your home when you're away

Some tips for outsmarting burglars when you're on vacation:

How photoelectric sensors work

 Light sensor turns light on at dusk and off at dawn.

For outdoor lights, the sensor is typically packaged in an outdoor weatherproof box attached to floodlights for house or driveway.

Sensor can be operated by a switch or attached to a timer, which can be set to turn the floodlights on and off.

 House lights
- Put an automatic timer on at least two lights.

 Radios, answering machines
- Put an automatic timer on a radio.
- Never leave answering machine messages that indicate you're away from home.

 Newspapers
- Stop delivery.

 Mail
- Have the post office hold your mail or ask a neighbor to pick it up.

 Yard
- Hire a gardener or lawn service if you'll be gone more than a week.

 House watch
- Tell a neighbor or relative when you're leaving and returning; include itinerary and phone numbers where you can be reached.

SOURCES: National Crime Prevention Council, Bureau of Justice Statistics, Alpine Electric Co.; research by PAT CARR

mally keep them that way; leave them in their normal positions.

❏ Consider leaving a car parked in the driveway to make the house look occupied.

❏ Lower or turn off the ringer on the telephone. That way burglars can't hear an unanswered phone.

❏ Don't announce that you are away on your phone

The Inside View: Tips from a House Burglar

Judy Amar was sentenced in 1988 to 10 years in prison after committing burglaries for five years, primarily in Palm Beach County, Fla., and netting an estimated $5 million in loot. From jail, she offered the following tips for preventing home burglaries:

☛ Get steel doors with steel frames. A break-in is fairly easy even with steel doors, if the frame is wood.

☛ Roll-down shutters will make your house a fortress.

☛ While dogs are good deterrents, snakes are better.

☛ Peruse your local hardware store. Among the home protection devices you'll find there are many types of screw assemblies that will prevent windows from being opened.

☛ Buy an imitation alarm panel plate; the amateur burglar won't be able to tell the difference. This could spare you the expense of buying a real alarm, she says.

☛ Consider a backup alarm system. Professional burglars know how to cut phone lines to deactivate the primary alarm system.

☛ Use infrared sensors, which detect body heat, to protect expensive displays such as art objects.

☛ Have alarms installed under carpeting.

☛ Remember: if someone really wants to get into your house, he or she will, though the better protected your home is, the less likely it is that you will be burglarized.

---

recorder message. If you're going to be gone for a long time, turn off the answering machine. People you care about know you're not home anyway.

Protecting Your Rental Apartment

As a renter, you don't have complete control over your apartment. But there are three aspects you should check out:

The apartment: Is there a deadbolt lock and peephole on the entry door? Will the lock be changed or rekeyed when you move in? Does the sliding glass door have a rod or bar in the lower track so it can't be opened, and pins or screws in the overhead frame so it can't be lifted out?

The building: Does the landlord or building manager tightly control all keys? Is there control over who enters and leaves the building? Are background checks conducted on these people? Are walkways, entrances, parking areas, elevators, hallways, stairways, laundry rooms and storage areas well-lighted 24 hours a day? Are fire stairs locked from the stairwell side above the ground floor, so you can exit but no one can enter? Are mailboxes in a well-traveled, well-lighted area, and do they have good locks? Is the building well-maintained? Does it have functioning lights and trimmed landscaping?

The neighbors: Get to know them. Join or organize an Apartment Watch group. Consider a tenant patrol that watches for crime around the building, escorts elderly residents or those with physical disabilities, and monitors the lobby. Work with landlords or managers to sponsor social events for tenants. Consider causes of problems: Could a social evening for teens, a tenant association or a new playground help minimize the threat of crime?

Tips for the Elderly

The key advice is to stay connected with friends, family and neighbors. From the home security perspective, that means letting neighbors know your schedule, and comings and goings.

❏ Consider setting a policy within your residential complex that requires a check on neighbors at least once a day.

❏ If you don't see a neighbor for a day or two, call or visit.

❏ Form a block club or neighborhood watch group. You'll meet people, and have an opportunity to target community concerns.

❏ Keep informed about neighborhood crime patterns or scams. Read your newspaper's police logs to stay up to date.

❏ Con artists often prey on senior citizens. Contact your Better Business Bureau, local building department, Department of Consumer Affairs or a professional association for information or to check companies.

❏ If a deal seems too good to be true, it usually is. Don't pay for work until it is done, and don't pay in cash if you can avoid it.

Two of every three burglaries in 1992 took place at residences. The average loss in a home burglary was $1,215. The average loss in a non-residential burglary was $1,400. (The FBI defines burglary as the unlawful entry of a structure to commit a felony or theft.)

Eighty-seven percent of burglaries in 1992 were never solved.

An estimated 2.98 million burglaries took place in the United States in 1992—one burglary every 11 seconds, according to the FBI. Still, that's down by 7 percent from 1988 and down 5 percent from 1983.

2

Crime-Proofing Yourself

Making yourself crime-proof—on the streets, in your car, in the mall or at work—doesn't have to be daunting.

People who are crime-proof carry their wallets and purses defensively. They use cellular phones, CB radios and alarms. They know their neighbors. And they try not to appear confused, lost or uncertain, the kind of attitude that attracts crime.

Eve Levin knows. "I love to walk around at night," says the 30-year-old San Francisco resident. "And I hadn't felt like I could do that for years." Fed up with feeling afraid, she took steps to improve her personal security. Now when she runs out of ingredients in the middle of a recipe, she doesn't hesitate to walk to the store, even at night.

"Awareness is the name of the game," says Gary Denney, regional director of Citizens Against Crime in Philadelphia. "We give criminals the opportunity to accomplish crime, and we have to learn how to cut down on those opportunities."

And opportunities abound: one criminal offense occurs every two seconds in the United States, according to FBI statistics for 1992 (the latest available). A property crime occurs every three seconds, a robbery every 47 seconds and a murder every 22 minutes.

"We're strapped for manpower," says Robert Joseph, crime prevention officer for Lake County police in Gary, Ind. "We can't be in your neighborhood all the time. Because of that, you have to take some of that responsibility."

Walking

Crimes involving face-to-face confrontations with a criminal, even in your own neighborhood, are of great concern today. A 1992 Gallup Organization survey asked Americans: "Is there any area within a mile of your home where you would be afraid to walk alone at night?" Forty-four percent said yes.

The first step is acknowledging your vulnerability. "If you believe you are a potential victim, you will automatically take precautions," says Joan McKenna, president and founder of Women Against Rape in Collingswood, Pa. "The more precautions you take, the less likely you are to be a victim." When McKenna goes out, for instance, she keeps her keys in her hand and looks around her car to see if anyone is hanging around. In short, she's alert.

The way a person carries himself or herself says a great deal to a thief. He looks for women who keep their eyes on the ground while their purse bounces against their waist. Other targets are people distracted by small children, loud music on headphones or abundant shopping bags.

"Before you leave the house, take a look at yourself and

How to spot larceny-theft

Larceny-theft is stealing someone else's property without using force, violence or fraud.

Most thefts are from motor vehicles

Types of theft, in percent of total:

From motor vehicles **23%**

Purse-snatching **1%**
Pocket-picking **1%**
Coin machines **1%**
Bicycles **6%**
From buildings **14%**
Motor vehicle accessories **14%**
Shoplifting **16%**

Other **24%**

Most thefts occur in the heat of the summer

Percent of larceny-thefts by month, 1992

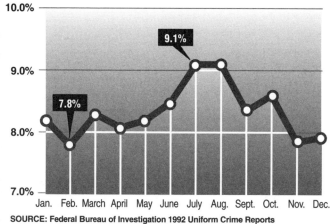

9.1%

7.8%

10.0%

9.0%

8.0%

7.0%

Jan. Feb. March April May June July Aug. Sept. Oct. Nov. Dec.

SOURCE: Federal Bureau of Investigation 1992 Uniform Crime Reports

see your vulnerable points," says Officer Anita Johnson of the Chester, Pa., police department. "Don't go out with your gold all hanging out, or your pocketbook hanging loose. Don't leave your car running while you run in the house. Watch what you wear, try to stay away from places that are not well-lit, travel with a buddy."

Keep the following tips in mind, and use them as you find appropriate:

❏ There's safety in numbers. Walk near other people on well-traveled paths and sidewalks. Don't take desolate short-cuts, no matter how tempting.

❏ Walk confidently. Wear a look of complete assurance. That look should say to people, "Don't trifle with me."

❏ Stay away from doorways, where strangers can lurk unseen. Walk down the middle of the sidewalk. If you feel really threatened, consider walking down the middle of the street. Robbers are less likely to approach you if you're making yourself conspicuous.

❏ Don't use a pay phone in a secluded area. Find one that has good lighting and plenty of foot traffic.

❏ Watch out for people in crowds who bump into you or let money fall at your feet so you'll bend over. They could be pickpockets who use distraction to carry out their deed.

❏ Avoid pricey clothes, jewelry and furs that announce that you are an attractive target. In other words, don't advertise your bank account.

❏ Women, leave the stiletto heels in the closet. Wear low heels that will make it easier for you to run from an attacker, if necessary.

❏ If you think you're being followed, turn and look straight at the stranger to let him know you're alert. It may make you feel more confident now that the person knows

How to be street smart

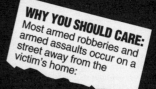

Some tips for protecting yourself from robbery or assault while you're walking or jogging:

The big three

- Stay alert.
- Walk or run confidently.
- Trust your instincts; if you feel uncomfortable in a place or situation, leave.

Choose busy streets

- Avoid passing vacant lots or construction sites.
- Stick to well-lighted areas at night.

Don't walk or jog alone

- Go with a friend or take your dog.

Know your neighborhoods

- Learn what stores and restaurants are open late and where police and fire stations are located.

Dress sensibly

- Carry purse close to your body and grip it firmly.
- Carry wallet in an inside coat pocket or front trouser pocket.
- Don't overload yourself with parcels.
- Avoid wearing shoes or clothing that restrict your movements.

Evading Purse Snatchers

Decide whether you must carry a purse, or whether you're using one sheerly from habit.

Consider not carrying a purse. Try these ideas:

☛ Trade your purse for a waist pack. Clean out your bulging wallet and carry only the essentials.

☛ Buy clothing that has adequate pockets.

If you can't live without your purse:

☛ Hold your purse firmly. Cover the clasp with your hand.

☛ Don't let your purse hang loosely from your shoulder.

☛ Put your handbag in your lap when sitting in public.

☛ Don't put your purse on the floor. Don't hang it on the door in public restrooms.

☛ Never leave your purse unattended in a shopping cart.

☛ To prevent having your wallet snatched, keep your purse closed at all times, particularly in crowds.

For more information, see Chapter 3 on crime-proofing for women.

---

you have committed his face to memory. Then change directions. Cross the street and mix up the speed of your pace, if your follower is on foot. If the stranger is driving a car, immediately turn around and walk in the opposite direction to give him the slip.

❏ Still uneasy? Go to a store, fire station or another safe public place nearby. A police station would be ideal, but any busy, well-lighted place will do. Get help, shout or phone someone if you feel that your actions have not discouraged the stranger. In some cities and on some college campuses, police or security departments offer escorts as a public service.

❏ Carry only what you need with you. Clean out your

wallet. Leave at home credit cards you don't use frequently, your voter registration card and other seldom-needed items.

❏ Don't carry a wad of cash. When you take out your wallet, keep your money hidden. Put away your change quickly.

❏ If you're carrying a purse, hug it under your arm against your side, with your hands over the clasp.

❏ Men: Carry your wallet in your front pocket or an inside jacket pocket. Instead of a wallet, try carrying a few bills in a money clip that fits into your pocket.

In a Car

Criminals often approach motorists to take their valuables. While it's upsetting to lose your belongings, the confrontation over the car, the wallet, the briefcase or the purse may put you at personal risk, physically or psychologically.

Some things to remember when you're driving:

❏ Lock the doors. Make it a habit to keep them locked at all times. Train your kids to lock their doors, too. At stoplights in some urban areas, thieves try to open the passenger door to steal your purse or briefcase.

❏ Keep the windows closed. You're probably safe with open windows on a country road, but not in the city.

❏ Always leave enough room when you stop behind a car to pull around it.

❏ Don't pick up hitchhikers. Conversely, don't hitchhike, and don't accept rides from strangers.

❏ Consider having your car windows coated with a special film that keeps glass from flying apart easily. Closed windows are one barrier between you and the bad guys, but windows can be broken. In some cities, thieves have taken to shattering car windows with tiny ceramic spark plugs. Even if thieves get your money, the window film may protect you and your passengers from being cut. Auto windows today no longer break in shards, but you can still be hurt by flying nuggets of glass.

❑ Keep valuables in the trunk or otherwise hidden.

❑ When you leave your car, be sure to lock it. Don't forget to take your keys.

❑ Park in a parking spot that will be lighted when you return. If you feel uneasy, ask someone to escort you—either a security guard or someone you trust.

❑ Have your keys ready in your hand, not in your pocket or purse, when you get in or out of your car.

❑ Glance underneath your car and look under surrounding vehicles to see if anyone is hiding there.

❑ Peer into the backseat to see if anyone is hiding before you drive away. Robbers have been known to hide inside a car, awaiting your return. Push the front seat forward when you park your car to make it easier to see the backseat.

❑ Consider buying a cellular phone. You'll be able to call for a tow truck or other help if you break down. You'll also be able to call the police if you encounter a dangerous situation.

❑ Mount compact disc players, cassette tape machines and CB radios out of sight, if possible. Take your cellular phone with you. If the theft of car radios is common in your area or thieves are attracted to your type of car, look into removable car radios that you can pull out and lock in the trunk after parking.

Please refer to Chapter 6 for a fuller discussion on staying safe in your car.

Using Public Transportation

Two words: be alert.

Be sure you have correct change for the bus, subway or

train before you leave home. That way you won't have to approach strangers to make change in a crowded station.

In the bus or train station, do not let anyone single you out of the crowd. Do not respond if someone who makes you uncomfortable asks you for the time. Stay close to other people. Try to wait at busy, well-lighted stops.

On the bus, sit across from the bus driver—not near the rear exit. Or sit in an aisle seat.

If a stranger bothers you, go ahead and yell.

Taxi Tips

Sit in the back of the taxi, not in the front seat.

Carry money in a variety of denominations. In an ideal world, the driver should be willing to break a $20 bill for you. But if he or she won't or can't, you expose yourself to danger if you have to plead for change on the street.

Note the driver's hack license number, and nonchalantly work it into the conversation to show you noticed it. Perhaps say, "Geez, 1943, that was the year I was born."

When you hand the money to the driver, be sure to place it in his hand, not on the seat. Thieves can snatch fare money while the door or window is open.

Returning Home

If you're driving, check your rearview mirror. If you're on foot, check to see if you were followed. Is there someone lurking near your driveway? If you think you're being followed, go to a safe place. Don't lead a criminal to your home.

Don't fumble with the house keys in a darkened doorway. Instead, have your keys ready as you walk up to the door. If you hear something suspicious and fear a thief is inside, don't go in the house. Call police from a neighbor's phone or cellular phone.

If you use an automatic garage door opener, check that a criminal didn't slip into the garage while you drove in. Look around before you get out of the car or close the garage door.

See Chapter 6 for more details about driveway crime.

Answering the Door

Before you open the door, know who's on the other side. When the doorbell rings, peer through the peephole to see who's there. (Install a peephole if you don't have one.)

This is a tougher rule to follow than you think. How many of us have opened the door to a stranger based on the impression that the caller doesn't look dangerous? To someone bearing an express package? To a child selling Scout cookies or raising money for the school band?

Use your judgment: keep the door closed if you're not sure. The chain guard alone won't keep out determined thieves.

Ask service people to slide their identification badge under the door. If you're concerned, call their office to verify identification.

If someone asks to use the phone, don't let the person inside. Instead, offer to make the call for him or direct him to a pay phone.

At the ATM

With the proliferation of automatic teller machines across the nation, ATMs have become a way of life, convenient and easy to use. And as their numbers grow, so do ATM-related crimes—whether it's people being robbed at cash machines or thieves using stolen bank or credit cards to withdraw money.

State and local governments are moving to regulate ATM security, setting standards for lighting, landscaping and security. Banks, too, are taking more action to protect their customers. They're enclosing ATMs in vestibules, shutting down some machines after dark and hiring security guards.

Police say ATM safety depends on common sense. "If people use normal precautions and are aware of what's going on around them, they shouldn't be in any trouble," says Sgt. Jim Hurley, robbery squad supervisor with Fort Lauderdale Police.

Some safety tips:

❏ When selecting your secret code, don't use any number or word that can be found in your wallet, such as your birth date, address or phone number.

❏ Keep your secret code secret. Memorize your code; don't write it down. Don't tell anyone your number.

❏ Never lend your card to anyone. Treat your ATM card as if it were cash.

❏ Be aware of your surroundings, especially at night. Look for suspicious people or activity around the ATM.

❏ Have your ATM card and completed forms ready in your hand as you approach the machine.

❏ When you enter your secret code, use your body as a shield so no one can see the numbers.

❏ If you notice anything out of the ordinary, even if you've already started a transaction at the machine, cancel the transaction and leave the area. Come back later, or use another ATM.

How to protect yourself at ATMs

Some tips for protecting yourself from robbery while using an automatic teller machine:

WHY YOU SHOULD CARE: In 10 years, the number of ATMs, ATM transactions and ATM cards issued has more than doubled.

General tips

- If you notice anything unusual, leave – even if you've already started a transaction.
- To safeguard account information, take your receipt with you.
- Don't count or display your money at ATM.
- If you have problems with ATM, leave and contact bank; don't accept offers of help from strangers.

Using ATMs at night

- Try to take a companion along.
- Park close to the ATM; park in a well-lighted area.
- If the lights aren't working at an ATM, don't use that machine.

Protecting your secret code

- Memorize your secret code; don't tell it to anyone or write it down.
- Don't pick a secret code that uses any number or word that can be found in your wallet (birth date, address, phone number, etc.).
- When entering your code, use your body to shield the numbers.

SOURCE: Long Beach Press-Telegram

Surveys show:

❏ About 50 percent of ATM crimes occur between 7 P.M. and midnight.

❏ December is the peak time for ATM use—and for ATM crimes.

❏ Customers are injured in about 14 percent of the crimes.

❏ Don't accept offers of help from anyone you don't know. If you have problems with the machine, leave and contact your bank later.

❏ Do not count money as you walk away from the machine. Put it away immediately and count it when you get to a safe place. If there's a mistake, report it to the bank as soon as you can.

❏ Take your receipt or transaction records with you—to keep your account information confidential.

❏ Roll up passenger windows and lock doors at a drive-up ATM. Leave space between your car and the car in front of you so you can drive around it, if necessary.

Avoid using an ATM at night, if you can. Plan ahead. But if you must, use precaution when approaching an ATM at night: park close to the machine in a well-lighted area. If the lights at an ATM are not working, don't use it.

At the Mall

Every Christmas, police and store managers alert the public to holiday thieves. But keeping safe in a shopping district is a year-round responsibility. "People shouldn't be lulled into a false sense of security just because they're in a mall," says Keith Foxe, a spokesman for the International Council of Shopping Centers. "They should be as alert in the mall as they are in other public places."

Most common threat inside the mall: pickpockets. Be alert, especially in crowded areas. "The minute you get bumped, check your wallet right there," says Sgt. Michael Gallagher, of the Metro Police Department in Dade County, Fla.

Thieves sometimes travel in groups, employing as many as eight people to make a single robbery go smoothly. They work like this: One thief gets the wallet out of a victim's purse or pocket—and passes it to another. The wallet is passed rapidly away from the scene, usually out of the mall to a waiting car. Even if the first pickpocket is identified by witnesses, the evidence is long gone.

Be aware of distraction theft. Someone who asks you for change, directions, the time or information may be trying to distract you while an accomplice takes your wallet. Other distractions are more dramatic: faking an illness, or spilling food or a drink on you.

Even in grocery stores, thieves have been known to place their items in another cart and pretend to be mistaken. While the shopper helps put the items in the correct cart, someone steals the victim's wallet.

"Malls are still pretty safe," says Terry Lewis, general manager of Carolina Place Mall in Pineville, N.C. "We do have security, but you can never get too complacent. People have got to help themselves."

Some tips:

❑ Plan your trip and carry only the necessary credit cards or cash.

❑ Do not wear expensive jewelry.

❑ Don't leave your purse in a shopping cart, and don't hang it off the handles of an infant stroller. A thief can whisk it away before you could react.

❑ Remember where you are parked. If you forget, go to

the mall's information desk or hospitality suite to get a security escort. The potential for personal harm is greater in parking lots than in the mall itself.

❑ Put packages in the trunk of your car.

❑ Avoid parking near oversized vehicles that reduce your visibility and your ability to see who's around you.

❑ If you shop after dark, use valet parking or find a space in a well-lighted area or near an entrance. Avoid walking to your car alone.

❑ In parking lots, have your keys in your hand. Walk briskly and with a purpose. Don't wander around like you're lost.

❑ Keep your keys in a pocket, not in your purse. That way, if someone steals your purse, you won't lose your car, too.

❑ If you see someone suspicious, go back to the store or shopping center and alert security.

❑ Once in your car, immediately lock the doors.

At Work

Until recently, many of us never thought of crime affecting us in the workplace. However, it's clear that a place of business is attractive to thieves—and you don't have to work in a high-visibility business such as bank or a convenience store to become a victim.

Your objective is to protect yourself, your personal property and company property against criminals.

The key to protecting yourself from robbery or assault at work is the same as it is on the street: Stay alert. Use common sense.

Be careful when using stairwells or restrooms that are accessible to the public.

Keep your purse or wallet locked in a drawer or closet.

How to make your workplace safe

Some tips for protecting yourself against robbery or assault at your place of business:

WHY YOU SHOULD CARE:

In 1992, more than 900,000 burglaries took place at stores, offices and other nonresidential buildings.

- Protect all openings and roof areas with burglar bars, steel mesh wires or an alarm system.

- Consider installing a surveillance camera.

If you're working late

Try to arrange your schedule so you'll be working with another employee.

Ask the security guard or a co-worker to escort you to the parking lot or a cab.

When strangers appear

Get identification from delivery or repair people who want to enter a restricted area or take equipment.

Check the identification of strangers who ask for confidential information.

Call security or the police if you notice anyone suspicious.

Personal safety

Keep your purse or wallet in a locked drawer or closet at all times.

Be extra cautious when using stairwells or restrooms that are open to the public.

Office safety

Keep emergency numbers for security, police and fire assistance posted near phones.

Never write down a safe or vault combination or a computer password.

SOURCES: National Crime Prevention Council, Bureau of Justice Statistics, Long Beach Press-Telegram; research by PAT CARR

Don't write down a safe or vault combination. Also, don't write down a computer password.

Keep emergency numbers for security, police and fire assistance posted near phones.

Get identification from delivery or repair people who want to enter a restricted area or remove equipment. Check the IDs of any stranger who asks for confidential information.

Call your company's security department or the police if you notice anything suspicious.

If you're working late, try to coordinate your schedule with another employee so you're not alone.

At night, ask a security guard or co-worker to walk with you to the parking lot or a cab.

Employee Violence

Violence in the workplace, particularly that committed by a disgruntled employee, is a growing concern.

Workplace violence may be directed at co-workers or supervisors. It can include spreading vicious rumors, exchanging angry words, making direct or indirect threats, stalking, harming property, sabotaging equipment and committing arson and assault.

Pay attention. "About 99 percent of the time, people make threats before committing violence at work," says Michael Goodboe, vice president of Wackenhut Corp. in Coral Gables, Fla. Stay alert to these warning signs of a potentially violent person. He or she:

❏ Is often a loner, with no family or friends. The job is the person's life—the primary source of identity and connection to people. The fear of losing this job can tip him or her over the edge.

❏ Has a migratory job history. Employee frequently

changes jobs and often has serious disregard for company policies; constantly challenges authority.

❏ Is chronically disgruntled: the employee is in a constant state of anger, does not work well with others, blames everyone else for his or her mistakes, and accepts no responsibility for his or her bad luck.

❏ Is influenced by violence and fascinated by it.

❏ Uses drugs or alcohol.

A person contemplating violence often gives warning signs in advance, or cries out for help in other ways. Examples include suicide threats or threats against a co-worker or supervisor, talking about a special plan "to solve everything," or paranoia and irrational behavior.

Most important, be aware it can happen anywhere. Notify a responsible person if you become worried about a co-worker.

On Elevators

When the doors of an elevator close, you have no choice about the company you're keeping. "Follow your gut instinct," says Joan McKenna, of Women Against Rape in Collingswood, Pa. "If you are in an elevator and get a bad vibe about somebody there, get out of there. Women are basically sensitive and don't want to hurt someone's feelings." But it's better to hurt a potential attacker's feelings than get into a situation where you could be hurt. "You can say, 'Oh, I forgot my book,' and get off. Or don't say a word. We don't owe anybody an explanation for protecting ourselves."

Some other tips:

❏ Join a crowd of people when getting on the elevator. There's safety in numbers.

❏ Stand clear of the door while waiting for an elevator to arrive. This prevents a bad guy from pulling you in.

❏ Check inside before entering. Are you uncomfortable with the people you see? Wait for the next elevator.

❏ Stand by the push-button control panel. This keeps you in the elevator "driver's seat." Note the location of the alarm button.

❏ Get off the elevator if you feel uncomfortable with the other passengers.

❏ If someone starts to attack you on the elevator, push all the buttons except the red one that stops the elevator. Hit the alarm button.

On the Path to Fitness

You can crime-proof yourself even when you strap on your running shoes or mount your bicycle. Some tips from the National Crime Prevention Council and other experts:

❏ Go with a friend.

❏ Vary your route and your timing. This prevents someone from waiting for you, or from robbing your home while you're away.

❏ Stay away from desolate neighborhoods—especially at night. Avoid parks or streets without lighting, for example.

❏ Keep alert. That means keeping the volume down on the headphones.

❏ Take a cellular phone with you so you can call for help. Or carry change so you can make a call from a pay phone.

What to Do During an Attack or Robbery

Faced with a criminal, how should you react? The main thing to remember is that your goal is to escape.

There are a number of ways to accomplish this. You can try to distract your attacker. Among the tactics are throwing up or relieving yourself, telling him you see your spouse or the police coming, or saying you're pregnant or have AIDS.

"Be creative with your story line," says Frances Taylor, crime-prevention officer with the Mecklenburg County, N.C., police. "I've also heard of circumstances where female victims laughed hysterically or cried hysterically, and that changed the mind of the individual."

Sometimes, staying calm and reasoning with an attacker is a good option.

Yelling is also suggested. But shout, "Help! Fire!" Don't scream, "Help! Police!" Bystanders may be more likely to come running to see a fire, if only to protect their own property.

Show your money to your attacker and say, "This is all I have." Then throw it in one direction—and run the other way. Shout, "Help! Fire! Help!" Most of the time, the thief will take the money and not go after you.

If the criminal grabs you, yank on his thumb and try to break it. If he grabs your coat, try to slip out of it and run. Don't try to win. Just buy yourself enough time to get away, or to attract help.

Defensive Measures

Some people consider carrying a non-lethal weapon such as pepper spray, tear gas spray, a baton, or even an umbrella. But there are drawbacks to these approaches: the weapon must be immediately accessible, and you must be knowledgeable and prepared to use it. Police also worry that these self-defense products impart a false sense of self-confidence, or that they can be used against the person carrying them or innocent bystanders. (See Chapter 7 on weapons.)

The best approach is to be alert and avoid assault. If a criminal confronts you, you should attempt to escape. But if you are in danger of bodily assault and are forced to defend yourself against an assault, and you have chosen not to carry a self-protection device, here are a few useful moves:

The "key strike." Hold your keys tightly between your fingers and punch sharply at your assailant's eyes and face. Or hold a key solidly between the thumb and forefinger and sweep it across the assailant's eyes.

The "foot stomp." This sometimes can work well when someone attacks you from behind. Quickly look down and to one side to aim your blow—then pound your heel or edge of your shoe on the top of your assailant's foot. This can be devastating with high-heeled shoes. A crushing heel stomp throws your assailant off balance. Run away immediately, or follow up with a second strike such as grabbing, twisting, squeezing and pulling your attacker's genitalia.

The "eye strike." This move cuts off your attacker's vision. Extend all the fingers of one hand, with palm curved slightly. Gouge attacker's eyes deeply, as hard as possible. Flee or follow up with a second strike such as a groin kick.

The "groin kick." This move can be a good follow-up to a strike to the throat or eye, especially if the attacker has grabbed your wrist. It's not good as an initial move because many men expect it and move easily out of the way. Your knee is the usual weapon, but depending on your distance from the attacker, you can use a shin or foot. Kick powerfully—that is a must to be effective. Visualize yourself lifting him a foot off the ground with your wallop.

The "knee kick." This move can help if you're attacked

How victims of violent crimes protect themselves

Some evidence based on Justice Department interviews with crime victims between 1973 and 1992:

Most victims take steps to protect themselves...

Approximate percent of victims who take some measure to protect themselves, by type of crime.

All violent crimes	71%
Rape	82%
Robbery	58%
Assault	73%

...and most think defensive steps helped them

Outcome of protective measures reported by victims, in percent.

Helped them	71%
Hurt them	7%
Both helped and hurt	6%
Neither helped nor hurt	11%

Resisting or capturing offender is most frequently cited measure

Top five defenses used by victims, in percent.

23%	Resisted or captured offender
16%	Ran away or hid
14%	Persuaded or appeased offender
12%	Attacked offender without a weapon
11%	Got help or gave alarm

Defensive steps save property, but increase risk of injury

Percent of armed robberies (handgun) that resulted in property loss.

56%	When victims defended themselves
89%	When victims took no action

Percent of armed robberies (handgun) that resulted in personal injury

25%	When victims defended themselves
6%	When victims took no action

SOURCES: National Crime Prevention Council, Bureau of Justice Statistics, International Association of Fire Chiefs; research by PAT CARR

from behind and your assailant's groin is beyond reach. Lift one leg, then kick backward toward your attacker's knee or shin. Experts say to visualize driving your heel through your target. Turn your head so you can aim at either the front or side of the knee. Run away immediately.

It's helpful to know the vulnerable points on your assailant's body: temples, eyes, nose, jaw, chin, side of neck, throat. Lower on the body, they are the solar plexus, ribs, abdomen, groin, knees, shin and instep.

After a Crime Occurs

What do you do if you've just become a crime victim?

Chances are you're pretty shaken and will feel that way for some time. Even so, call 911 right away.

Most communities today have 911 emergency systems, though there are still small towns where dialing 911 doesn't work and that could delay getting help to your side. If you're in a strange town, look on the pay phone for the local emergency police number. You don't want to slow police response time in an emergency.

Generally, this is what will happen when you phone in an emergency.

First, the operators will ask for your name and the phone number you're dialing from. This information is critical in case you get disconnected or someone cuts you off.

Don't take it personally if the stream of questions coming from the emergency operator sounds cool and detached. Operators are trying to get as much information as fast and as clearly as possible. More than likely, they're relaying that information to officers who are en route.

"Take a deep breath," says Steve Garcia, an officer with the Downey, Calif., police department, "and tell us what's happening. We need to get that information quickly. The less time you waste, the better chance we have of catching the guy."

When you call 911, the system automatically records the address you're calling from, but the police still need to get that information from you to double-check it, or in case you're calling from somewhere other than the crime scene.

If you need medical treatment, say so. Even if you think your injuries are not serious, you could have problems later or need a record of them.

Once you've taken care of your own safety and the safety of those around you, start writing things down.

If you saw the suspect, jot down your impressions of what the person was wearing, how the person looked and any special features you noticed: scars, tattoos, moles, beard, mustache, limp. The more specific, the better.

Don't simply give the race, gender and height of the person because that could apply to thousands of people. "But a gold tooth and a strange accent and an uneven mustache," says Garcia, "these are things that are a little more specific."

If you have been attacked, try not to become frustrated if you can't remember much.

The police are relying on you to be your own witness, but they haven't forgotten that you're also the victim.

"You can be so traumatized that it's lost in your head for a while," says Officer Bob Anderson of the Long Beach Police Department. "One person can have a violent attack and everything is in slow motion without faces, whereas another can notice a scar."

If you're having trouble remembering, chances are you'll recall events later.

Make sure there is a written police report of the crime and

Describing an assailant

If a crime occurs use this chart right away to list as much information on the suspect as you can remember.

Sex _____

Race _____

Age _____

Height _____

Hair color _____

Eye color _____

Scars or marks _____

Hat (color, type, etc.) _____

Shirt _____

Tie _____

Coat _____

Pants _____

Shoes _____

What police want to know when you report a crime

■ **Your name and phone number:** Police need this information immediately in case you're disconnected.

■ **Location, possible injuries and other basic facts:** Remain calm and speak as clearly as possible; the emergency operator may be relaying the information to officers while you are on the line.

■ **Description:**
Here's the best order when describing people:
Sex
Race
Age
Height
Weight
Build
Hair
Clothing
Complexion
Identifying marks

■ **Vehicles:**
Here's the best order in describing vehicles:
Color
Make
Body type
License number
Direction of travel
Number of occupants
Identifying marks

SOURCES: Press-Telegram

REGINALD MYERS / The Herald

that you get the report number. These documents will make it easier to file claims, qualify for aid and seek restitution.

Ask the police officers whether you can look at file photos of criminals to see if you recognize your assailant.

How You'll Feel Afterward

About 14.4 million criminal offenses were reported in 1992, of which nearly two million were violent crimes, according to FBI statistics. If you are a victim, your experience can leave you feeling shaken and traumatized.

Don't hesitate to take advantage of support groups in your community. Ask your local police department about victim and witness programs. The courts or probation departments often have information about victim restitution payments, and the prosecutor's office can answer questions about how the judicial system works.

Call community crisis hotlines for referrals to counseling groups. Getting involved with Crime Watch or neighborhood anti-crime groups can also help you feel more empowered and in control of your life.

Despite a slight decline in crime in 1993, a Gallup poll found fear of crime is the nation's No. 1 concern. It's never been higher since Gallup began checking in the 1930s.

A 1991 survey by the National Victim Center found that respondents were fearful of being attacked while traveling (72 percent), or out alone at night in their neighborhoods (61 percent), or at home in their own house or apartment (60 percent). Women were particularly apt to change their lives in order to avoid crime—limiting the places they go by themselves, for example.

The total number of crimes in 1992: 14,438,191. The good news: that's down 2.9 percent from 1991.

Violent crimes occur most frequently in summer, and least often during winter.

Regions with the most violent crime:
The South, 37 percent
The West, 25 percent
The Northeast, 19 percent
The Midwest, 19 percent

There were 23,760 murders in 1992, down 3.8 percent from 1991.

The average loss in a robbery in 1992 was $840, up from $817 in 1991, according to the FBI. Included are robberies of banks and convenience stores.

3

Crime-Proofing for Women

When Jennifer Calderin leaves her home in Davie, Fla., she straps on a wrist alarm intended to deafen an attacker. She carries a cellular phone to call for help. She won't go anywhere without her husband after dark.

Just across town, Viorika Spariosu blithely walks home from her night job at a Fort Lauderdale grocery store at 2 A.M., alone. "I see the news about what happens to people, but I don't worry about it," she says.

Two women, two approaches to crime. How can they be so different? On the paranoia meter, most women fall somewhere in the middle of the scale—neither paralyzed by, nor oblivious to, crime. But most women do grow up feeling more vulnerable than men, particularly on the streets and in the presence of people they don't know.

Ironically, strangers hurt far more men than women. The reason: women may be more careful than men, taking more precautions to keep themselves from becoming crime victims.

What that means is that a woman is far more likely to be hurt by someone she knows than by a stranger. More than 70 percent of physical assaults on women occur when they try to leave boyfriends or husbands, according to the U.S. Justice Department. Seventy-eight percent of rapes are committed by a man who the woman knows well, according to a National Victim Center survey.

The American Medical Association estimates that four million women a year are beaten by boyfriends or husbands, and roughly one in four women is likely to be abused by a partner at some time. Ninety-five percent of domestic violence involves female victims.

Here are some tips on how to avoid many crimes that commonly affect women, such as purse snatching.

Purse Snatching/Mugging

Purse snatching is not as frequent as it seems—representing only 1 percent of all larceny thefts, the FBI says. Would purse snatching be wiped out if women stopped carrying purses? Probably not totally. Pickpockets, who tend to prey on men, are just as active. Pocket picking also represents 1 percent of all larceny thefts.

Erma Bombeck likes to joke that whenever someone asks how old she is, she avoids the issue by saying, "I'm so old I can remember when you could safely hang your handbag on a hook inside a rest-room door." These days, thieves are apt to reach over the stall door to grab the purse and run.

While that's distressing, it's not as unsettling as having your purse torn from your shoulder while your attacker coolly ignores your protests. Like many robbery victims, women who have had their purses stolen in a one-on-one confrontation tend to recall the details with a particularly heightened sense. In fact, they may think of it as more than a loss of money, credit cards and keys—their minds linger on what potential violence might have transpired.

How to Prevent Purse Snatching

Purse snatching on the street can start as innocently as someone calling you over to ask for directions as a way to get you within reach. Or to ask you the time.

Keep a distance. Don't let people get too close, if possible. If someone who makes you feel uncomfortable asks you a question, keep walking.

When shopping for a purse, try it out for fit under your arm, not on your shoulder. To guard your purse, keep it closed, with your hand on the clasp and the opening turned toward your body. For extra protection, fold up the straps and carry it like a football. One alternative: wear a waist pack. A lot of women like to use a waist pack because it's compact and fits close to the body, reducing the chance of someone ripping it away.

However, if you feel fragile and worry about breaking bones, you may want to avoid waist packs. The force involved in stealing a waist pack by a determined thief could knock you down.

Another alternative: wear your coat over your purse. Try a tiny, slim purse that won't look bulky under the coat.

Alternative No. 3: follow the example set by men. Buy clothes with pockets. Carry only your driver's license, one charge card, one check, a photocopy of your car registration, auto club card, car insurance certificate, plus whatever you need for that outing. A rubber band will keep everything together and provide enough friction to keep it from sliding out of a pocket. Or keep the absolute necessities in a tiny change purse and relegate the makeup, comb, lip gloss and other accoutrements to a tote bag or briefcase.

Whatever you do, don't let your valuables dangle at your side in a shoulder bag, recommends Bob Portenier, a reformed ex-con who now gives crime prevention advice in Kansas.

When carrying packages, place your purse between the packages and your body so that it's out of sight. Don't attract attention by carrying or flashing large amounts of cash. After cashing a check, put the money in your purse before leaving the bank.

When using a public restroom, the most conservative approach is to dangle your handbag around your neck or balance it on your lap. Putting it on the floor or hanging it from the hook on the back of the door puts it within a thief's reach.

If you're approached by a purse snatcher, look for ways to escape. If that is impossible, don't fight back. A purse is not worth getting hurt over. Do not hang on to the purse, or you may get dragged on the pavement. Throw the bag in one direction and run in another. If you're worried about being thrown to the ground, toss the purse at the thief and sit down. (For more discussion on purse snatching, see tips on personal security in Chapter 2.)

Stalking

Maybe you know him, maybe you don't. Stalkers are not always known by their victims.

At first, he seems to be a real charmer. He sends imagi-

Right now around the country, an estimated 200,000 people are stalking ex-lovers, ex-bosses, celebrities, even strangers. In the first year of Florida's stalking law, 888 people were arrested for stalking and threatening to physically harm someone.

How to evade purse snatchers

The simplest way to foil purse snatchers is to stop carrying a handbag.

WHY YOU SHOULD CARE: The average financial loss in a purse snatching is $292, according to the FBI.

Handbag alternatives

Waist packs: Try trading your handbag for one of these; packs are safe, easy to wear and convenient, especially when you're walking, jogging or sightseeing.

Pockets: Buy clothing, particularly sportswear, with adequate pockets.

If you must carry a handbag. . .

✔ Hold it firmly and cover the clasp with your hand.

✔ Don't let your handbag hang loosely from your shoulder.

✔ Put your handbag in your lap when sitting in public places.

✔ Don't put your handbag on the floor; don't hang it on the door in public restrooms.

✔ Never leave your handbag unattended in a shopping cart.

SOURCE:
Federal Bureau of Investigation
1992 Uniform Crime Reports

native gifts, scribbles flattering prose and begs to be near you. But you're not interested.

When you tell him that, he won't accept it. He follows you everywhere—to work, to your home, to the grocery store. He makes threats . . . and now you are being stalked.

A first-time victim may view stalking as a sign of love. It isn't. It's a sign of power and control, whether the stalker is a former boyfriend or a complete stranger.

What you need to do is break all contact. Tell him: "Get

Profile of a Stalker

Florida police veterans Bob and Chuck Drago have studied stalking, especially among spurned-lover cases. A woman's rejection almost always is the trigger. A stalker tends to be insecure and can't tolerate rejection—real or perceived.

He acts in self-defeating ways. He drinks heavily or abuses drugs. He tries to recapture the object of his obsession with phone calls, letters, gifts. He may resort to emotional violence—canceling your credit cards, trying to sabotage your job, ordering a new roof for your house and leaving you with the bill.

Sometimes he threatens suicide and may even carry it out. "Very often they will say exactly what they're going to do, and then they do it," says Chuck Drago.

"They've always been deprived of power and a feeling of well-being and importance," says Dr. Bruce Danto, a Fullerton, Calif., forensic psychiatrist and former police officer. "They blame everybody else for their problems—the boss is no good, the car is no good, the pay is no good, the traffic is no good."

Stalkers tend to be loners—insecure people who are master manipulators. They seek to control or possess another person. Some stalkers develop a fascination for a certain celebrity or movie star, rather than for someone they know personally.

---

out of my life." Say it firmly, plainly, without question.

Call the police. An early arrest often interrupts a stalker's activity, keeping him from escalating to violence, even if he resumes some form of stalking after a trip to jail.

Almost all states have stalking laws. Michigan's law makes it a felony to relentlessly or maliciously pursue a person. Penalty: up to five years in prison and a $10,000 fine. You also have the right to sue your stalker. In Florida, the maximum penalty for stalking and making the victim fear bodily harm is five years in prison and a $5,000 fine.

Document everything. Keep all letters, tape all phone calls (if legal in your state), and keep a journal.

Tell friends, co-workers or supportive relatives about the problem. They could be your witnesses someday, plus provide a shoulder to lean on. Consider counseling. You may need help to deal with a stalker's pursuit.

Be security-conscious. Change locks. Change your phone to an unlisted number. Consider an alarm system. Don't leave work alone.

Develop a plan for worst-case scenarios so you're not stuck trying to think of a way out when confronted by a surprise encounter. Think of a way to get to a phone. Call a friend and use a seemingly innocuous code word to signal you're in trouble.

Acquaintance Rape

Stranger rape is relatively uncommon. Most rapes are committed by men who are familiar, even trusted. So-called date rape doesn't only happen on dates.

Listen to Bev Chrzanowski, who thought years of bodybuilding and martial arts made her invincible. But the owner of Spunky's Gym in Clawson, Mich., was nearly raped by an acquaintance during what began as a business meeting: "He had both my hands in one hand and all my clothes off in a matter of a minute." Chrzanowski managed to bloody his nose, then narrowly talked him out of raping her. Her escape burned two lessons into her brain: "So often it's a person you know," and "Don't expect to fight and win; you've got to escape."

If you find yourself in an uncomfortable or potentially threatening situation, begin by saying no. Say it loud and clear. Push away. Do not rely just on words to send the message. Let him know nonverbally, too. Leave. Go home.

You can take steps to prevent things from getting that far:

❏ Check a new date's background; ask friends about him.

❏ Drive yourself, or have a backup plan for getting home.

❏ Go with friends, if you don't know the man well. Make your limits clear. Avoid secluded places.

❏ Beware of drinking too much alcohol or taking drugs. They can cloud your judgment and diminish your ability to take appropriate action.

❏ Trust your instincts. If you feel uncomfortable, get away.

❏ Do not leave a party with someone you just met or don't know well.

If you are raped, get help. Immediately after an attack, call 911 and someone you trust to comfort you. Don't change your clothes, shower, douche, brush your teeth, eat or drink—or you could destroy evidence needed in court.

Why You Should Care
Seventy-eight percent of rapes are committed by a man who the woman knows well, according to a National Victim Center survey.

How to avoid date rape

Using care and common sense can help
women avoid being raped by men they know.

WHY YOU SHOULD CARE:
According to a National
Victim Center survey, 78%
of rapes are committed by
a man who knows the
woman well.

 Know the man you're dating: If
you have never been out with this
man before, ask friends about him.

 Plan how you'll get home:
Drive yourself or have a backup
plan to use in an emergency.

 **Avoid intimate situations with
strangers:** Go with friends if you don't
know the man well; avoid secluded
places.

 Draw the line: Make your
limits clear to your date.

 **Beware of drinking too much
alcohol or taking drugs:** Alcohol
and drugs can cloud your judgment
and weaken your ability to act wisely.

 Trust your instincts: If you feel
uncomfortable, get away.

 Use good judgment: Don't leave a
party or dance with someone you've
just met or don't know well.

SOURCE: Federal Bureau of Investigation
1992 Uniform Crime Reports

Call a rape hot line for counseling. If you are certain that you do not want to call police, then at least contact a rape treatment center for confidential medical treatment and counseling.

Victims of date rape tend to feel guilty and responsible. They think of how it sounds: Yes, I went to his apartment, but he was my friend. Yes, we had a couple of beers, but I trusted him. Yes, I wanted to kiss him—but that's different. But date rape cases can be prosecuted.

Stranger Rape

Rape by a stranger can never be construed as the victim's fault. At the heart of the attack is a desire for power and domination. It has nothing to do with uncontrolled sexual passions.

What a woman wears means nothing to a rapist. Neither does her age, nor who she is.

Once a rapist picks a potential victim, his next step is to test her to see if she's an easy target. He may start by asking the time or for directions. If the woman is overly polite, he may go on to make a threat.

Cars present the biggest potential danger. Do not walk up to a stranger in a car, or you could find yourself facing a weapon and ordered to get in. And once inside, your fate is sealed. "Never get in any vehicle with an armed criminal—at any time, for any reason," warns former convict Bob Portenier. "Your chances of survival go down drastically when you place yourself in a position of isolation."

Joan McKenna, of Women Against Rape in Collingswood, Pa., agrees: "When they say, 'Get in the car, or I'll kill you,' I don't know anyone who gets in the car and gets out OK. At least if you're outside, you've got the possibility of screaming."

Many rapes occur in or near the victim's home, so rape prevention begins with good home security. The Long Beach, Calif., police department suggests installing effective locks on all doors and windows—and using them. Lock your windows at night, no matter how hot it is. Be sure you know who's at the door before opening it. If someone comes to the door to deliver a package, ask him to leave it outside the door. If someone asks for help, tell him to wait outside while you phone for assistance. Don't put your first name on your mailbox. In the phone book, list only your initials and last name.

On foot, always walk a planned route on busy, well-lighted streets. Avoid desolate areas, especially at night. Carry a flashlight at night to signal for help, if needed. Be alert.

Do not hitchhike under any circumstances, and do not pick up hitchhikers.

When you're driving, lock your car doors and windows. Plan your route before going away so as not to get lost. Avoid parking in isolated areas; look for busy well-lighted spots. If you have car trouble, put on your emergency flashers and raise the hood. Tie a white cloth on your antenna or outside mirror. Then wait inside your car with the doors and windows closed. If someone stops, ask them to call police or a towing service. Do not accept an offer for a ride to the gas station.

Experts also suggest:

❏ Travel in groups. If you think you are being followed, run to a public place or the nearest home and call 911. Walk assertively—not slouched over with your head down.

❏ Carry a shriek alarm or whistle. Some police say a whistle is better than Mace or guns, which can be used against

and badge number of the responding officer and call a supervisor. "Women need to know that police won't always do what the law says they can do," says Susan McGee, executive director of the Domestic Violence Project in Ann Arbor, Mich. "Women must often take additional action—like fleeing. I know that's grossly unfair, but that's what women have to do for their own safety."

If the abuser is arrested, he will be taken to jail and held until he is released on bond, often within 24 hours.

Some women feel they will be in danger after the abuser is released. They should find a place where they (and their children) can feel safe—the home of a friend or relative, or a local shelter for battered women. Police, a local crisis

---

Once every 15 seconds in the United States a woman is beaten by her husband or boyfriend. Nearly a third of women murdered were killed by husbands or boyfriends, according to the FBI.

Battering is the single largest cause of injuries to women, according to the U.S. Surgeon General. Violence against females ages 15 to 44 is more common than auto accidents, muggings and cancer combined. Perpetrators overwhelmingly are male. Although assaults involving guns and knives are increasing, the weapons of choice are a man's fists.

What an abuse victim should take when she flees: prescription medication, glasses or contact lenses, insurance records, house and car keys, driver's license, credit cards, passport or voter registration, marriage license, Social Security numbers, financial information, birth certificates, immunization records and report cards.

---

you. Yell "Fire!" if you are attacked. Many people respond to that before they respond to a cry for police.

❏ Look in the backseat of your car before entering. Look underneath the car and those around it.

❏ If you return to your parked car and it has a flat tire, get help from the parking attendant or the office. Some attackers deliberately puncture women driver's tires, and then "coincidentally" offer to help you.

❏ Always carry your car or house key in your hand, ready to open the door.

What to Do If You're Attacked

Your best chance for escape is in the first moments, advises the Rape Treatment Center of Jackson Memorial Hospital in Miami. If you can't get away, your goal is survival.

There is no best way to react. You can scream, "Fire!" "No!" "Stop!" or make a ruckus. You can talk about something that interests you. You can say things to enhance his ego or suggest meeting at a better place and time. You could try to vomit, or tell your attacker you need to go to the bathroom right away. Don't cry or plead—this could excite him more.

You can stall by fighting back, but if you think you may be seriously injured or killed, then cooperate. Whatever you decide, your primary goal is to get out of this alive.

Ex-con Bob Portenier says that all women have the physical strength to manipulate the rapist and create an opportunity to get away. However, you may lack the mental toughness to pretend to relax and submit so he'll let go of your hands. If you're capable of doing this, you could gouge his eyeballs out with your fingernails or rip his testicles. "Do not allow a feeling of mercy or compassion to enter the thought process," he says. "The rapist feels nothing for the women and he should not be given any consideration."

The sex act ends in only one of two ways, says Portenier. "Either the rapist walks or drives away after the rape is over and the woman survives physically, or the rapist kills the woman to eliminate a witness. There are no other options in a rape termination. Every woman needs to be aware of this and decide what and how she will respond to a potential rape situation."

What should you do if it happens to you? The advice for dealing with the aftermath of stranger rape is the same for dealing with acquaintance rape. Consult the section on acquaintance rape for specifics.

Domestic Abuse

Domestic abuse is an age-old problem that only in recent years has come to be widely regarded as a crime.

Lawyers and counselors say domestic abuse victims should get immediate help. "He's doing it because nobody stops him," says David Garvin, director of Alternatives to Domestic Aggression in Ypsilanti, Mich., a counseling program.

The abuse victim should call 911 after the attack, or ask a sympathetic neighbor to call on her behalf. She should talk to a police officer alone—away from her abuser. In some states, police are allowed to make an arrest even if no criminal complaint is signed. All officers need are a description of what happened and some physical evidence of an assault.

If police do not take the complaint seriously, get the name

hotline or the United Way can provide a phone number for a shelter, where lodging, care and counseling may be available. Women should be aware, however, that not even a shelter offers total safety from a determined abuser.

Other women consider obtaining a restraining order saying their abuser is not allowed to enter their house, contact them or remove children. In some states, police now make note of all restraining orders on a statewide computer system.

If the abuser violates the restraining order, police should be called immediately. The abuser can be arrested and may face jail time and hefty fines.

Self-Defense: Should You Learn Martial Arts?

Good laws aren't enough to protect women, advocates say. The threat of crime has driven many women to take matters into their own hands.

Nightclub singer Kirsten Steinhauer studied karate because several men followed her to her Fort Lauderdale home after she left work at 4 A.M. Says Steinhauer: "You leave these classes with a sense of confidence because you feel like there's something you can do to protect yourself."

Should you learn karate or some other martial art? It depends. A good self-defense course can help you discern when to flee and when to fight back, instead of relying on knee-jerk responses.

"You have to use basic instincts. It depends on the person, on the situation," says Dean Kilpatrick, director of the Crime Victims Research and Treatment Center at the Medical University of South Carolina. If the attacker's intent clearly is to kill, you may as well resist, Kilpatrick says. "But some sadomasochists are inflamed to greater violence by resistance."

In the end, according to Kilpatrick, "it depends on the situation, and each woman faces a unique situation with unique circumstances."

How to Fight Off an Assault

The best defensive move against an assault is to avoid it in the first place. If, however, the threat of an assault looms, you have four choices, says Jaye Spiro, an expert in women's self-defense who teaches at Mejishi Martial Arts and Self-Defense Inc. in Detroit.

☛ You can flee—run away, drive off in a car.

☛ You can scream, curse, yell—the louder the better.

☛ You can use sirens, whistles, hot pepper sprays or other self-defense devices to attract attention or subdue an attacker.

☛ Or you can take a controversial route: use physical resistance, using your muscles or whatever object is handy, like an umbrella. However, remember that fleeing and yelling are far more effective than fighting back.

4

Crime-Proofing
Your Children

Things have changed noticeably since the days when parents grew up on "I Love Lucy" and 25-cent malts at the corner drugstore. Guns in schools. Sexual assaults. Missing children. All make the nightly news with astounding regularity.

What can you do to make kids aware of real dangers? You don't want to burden them with unnecessary worry, or make them hesitant to leave the house.

Children are quite receptive to crime-proofing information. What scares kids, police say, are not drug pushers and child snatchers. It's not knowing what to do. You can help them understand what to do and how to react.

Street-smart schooling begins in the stroller and carries through to high school. You can start with matter-of-fact conversations when your children are toddlers. "They can be taught to recognize and avoid potentially dangerous situations," says noted child psychologist Lawrence Balter. "When you see a group of aimless youths or people making a lot of noise, say, 'Those boys look like they're looking for trouble. Maybe we should cross the street.' "

But sitting tiny children down and lecturing them on the dangers that may lurk out there may send the message that they are helpless in the face of scary things. Instead, try to incorporate useful hints about busy intersections or suspicious people into your daily discussions about your children's surroundings. That will give them a sense that these are manageable situations.

Also, tell them how you have incorporated crime-proofing into your own routine. "It's important to let your child know what you're afraid of, so they will understand—and abide by—your request that they be home by the appointed time or that they call you when they reach their destination," says Joyce Reinitz, a psychiatric social worker in New York.

Don't ignore the issue of crime. Shielding children from reality is no solution. "To bury your head in the sand and say, 'My child could not be a victim' is to do your child a disservice," says TV crime show host John Walsh, whose son, Adam, disappeared from a South Florida shopping center in 1981. "You owe it to your child to give him the appropriate information."

Safety Tips to Teach Your Child

Finding ways to confront and explain social problems without robbing children of their innocence is a part of everyday life.

Here's how one woman resolved this issue: Patricia and Janet were walking their daughters home from school one afternoon as their 6-year-olds skipped ahead, lost in a game of ponies and princesses. At the end of the block, a grizzled man rose from his cardboard litter, swinging an empty bottle. The girls, oblivious, headed straight toward him. Janet yelled out: "Whitney, banana!" Whitney stopped in her tracks, grabbed her friend's hand and both girls ran back to their mothers.

"Banana?" Patricia asked.

"It's our code word," Janet explained. "Whitney and I both got tired of my constant lectures about street safety. Now, whenever I say 'banana,' she knows not to mess around or argue and comes straight back to me."

All families should have code words to signal when something is wrong, or simply to indicate whether it's safe to go with another adult, experts say.

You also should teach your child at a very young age how to use the telephone. It could be up to the youngster to get help fast during a fire or accident someday. Tell your child to dial 911. If you live in an area that doesn't have 911 service, teach your child to dial "0" for the operator.

The next step is also important: tell your child what will happen after the call goes through.

The dispatch operator will ask what's wrong. The child will be asked to give his or her full name and the address where the problem is occurring. This means your child must know facts like addresses, home phone number and your work number. It also helps if the child can describe your home, in case he or she gets lost.

Here are some more lessons kids should learn:

❏ Children should know their area code and how to make a long-distance call to specific relatives or family friends.

❏ Let them know that no one has the right to touch

them or make them feel uncomfortable, and that kids have the right to say, "No." Instruct your children to tell you if someone tries to touch them in an inappropriate way. Children rarely lie about these things.

❏ Ask them to tell you if a grown-up asks them to keep a secret.

❏ Play "what if." Ask children to think about hypothetical situations, such as, "What would you do if someone asked you to help look for his dog?" "What would you say if someone asked you for directions?" "What if someone tries to grab your arm?" Discuss the possible consequences of a wrong answer.

❏ Tell them that children should never walk alone. Develop a buddy system. Don't let young children ride their bicycles or skate by themselves.

❏ Teach your children that if they are followed or hassled, they should run where there are other people and cry or scream for help.

❏ Teach them to stay in busy, well-lighted places and to stay away from lonely corners. "Crimes take place in dark, deserted places," says officer Merri Pearsall of the New York Police Department Crime Prevention Unit.

❏ Tell kids to trust their instincts. If something feels funny, there's probably a good reason.

❏ Be matter-of-fact and calm in discussing personal safety with children. Don't teach fear. Teach facts and strategies.

Who Are Strangers?

Of course you've taught your kids to avoid strangers—people they don't know. But do they understand that a stranger also is anyone they don't know very well? A fa-

How to keep kids safe

Some tips for helping children protect themselves from crime:

What children should do if someone suspicious approaches them

WALK FAST OR RUN
to their home if someone is at home, to a neighbor's house or a safe house.

SCREAM FOR HELP, YELL,
make as much noise as they can.

What children should know

How to use the telephone
properly in case of emergency; have your child practice making emergency phone calls.

To refuse rides or gifts
from someone they don't know well.

Name, address, phone number,
including area code and parent's or guardian's work number .

To tell a trusted adult
immediately if anyone, even a close relative or teacher, touches them in a way that makes them feel uncomfortable.

To walk and play outside with friends,
not alone.

Never to play with guns, knives
or other dangerous objects or weapons.

SOURCES: National Crime Prevention Council, Bureau of Justice Statistics; research by PAT CARR

miliar face they see every day is not necessarily someone they know.

Many kids think of strangers as horrible monsters. They don't always realize that respectable-looking people can do harm, too. "A stranger doesn't look like a monster. He looks like any other person. Maybe he even looks like your mom and dad," police officer Brian Vandenburg in Schererville, Ind., teaches children through his department's Drug Abuse Resistance Education (D.A.R.E.) program.

Your children should learn that bad people may use tricks to get them to go away with them—say, by handing them candy or offering rides.

Tell kids to be watchful when they're in public, even with a friend. If someone tries to stop your child, the youngster should scream for help or make as much noise as possible. Tell kids to walk fast or run home (or to another safe house).

They should ignore someone asking for directions from

Lessons To Teach Your Children:

☞ "Never get into a car or go into anyone's home without Mom's or Dad's permission, and never go near a car with a stranger in it. If someone tries to force you to go somewhere, you should shout, 'I don't know you!' Run away or find a grown-up in a safe place."

☞ "Never tell someone on the phone that you are home alone. If you're alone, you should lock the door. Never open the door to any stranger. Tell the delivery man to leave the package outside."

☞ "Tell Mom or Dad right away if a stranger offers you a ride, candy, money or a gift or wants to take your picture."

☞ "If an adult tells you to keep a bad secret, you should tell a grown-up you trust."

---

a car. Help them understand that adults shouldn't be asking children for help.

If your child gets lost in a store, or feels troubled in any public spot, tell them to find a cashier, store clerk or security guard and ask for help.

Warn kids never to play with guns. Sometimes children find guns at friends' homes. Tell them if they see a gun, they should follow these steps: Stop. Don't touch. Leave the area. Tell an adult. Teenagers should do the same.

Safety Tips for Parents to Follow

While children can carry many security lessons with them, some safeguards fall squarely on parents' shoulders day in and day out.

Very important with small children: parents never should leave young children unattended—especially in the car or during a quick stop at the store.

When your child is older, stay aware of your child's activities. Question any gifts or money your child brings home. Keep an eye out for unusually strong bonds between an adult and your child. If your child doesn't like to be with someone, find out why.

The complex business of making a child's world safe is governed by one simple rule: get involved. "Support your Neighborhood Watch, and get into a strong network with your child's friends and their parents," says Cpl. Georgia Smith, a drug and alcohol prevention officer for the Long Beach, Calif., police. "Be aware of what the child is doing, watching and saying. . . . [Parents} need to know where their child is, and who they go around with."

Know who your child's friends are. Be sure you have their

addresses and phone numbers in your address book—and their parents' names and work numbers.

Establish call-in routines. For example, call from work when your child gets home from school. Have your son call you when he arrives at a friend's house and before he leaves. Have your daughter call home to say goodnight before bedtime at a sleep-over. Tell them to call when they're going to be late.

Take a good look daily at the clothes he or she is wearing. Forget monograms and personalized T-shirts. Keep your child's name off clothing, books and accessories. This prevents strangers from calling your child by first name. Kids assume anyone who knows their name must be their friend.

Don't let them carry a lot of money. But teach them always to have a quarter handy if they have to make a phone call for help or a ride home. Tell them how to call collect when they don't have money.

Most schools or child care centers have strict procedures as to who can pick up your child in your absence. Check to see that their information is up to date, and that they are following through with their own security procedures. If you have a judge's order transferring sole custody to you, be sure that the day care center or school has a copy in its files and that the staff is aware of it.

Always accompany your child to public bathrooms. If your child is older and doesn't want you to go with him or her, stand outside the main door until he or she comes out.

When your children go out at night, know where they are going and the time expected home. Jot down the license plate number if the trip is a joy ride with friends. If your youngster is going on a trip, write down the route he or she plans to take, who's going and who is the responsible adult.

In case of emergency, experts suggest you know how and where you can get copies of your child's medical and dental records. Have your child fingerprinted and keep the card in a safe place. Update your child's height and weight each year. Keep a current photo of your child.

Most of all, don't assume crime can't happen to your child.

Advice for Latch-Key Children

Millions of elementary school children are home alone each day after school. They can protect themselves.

Write down emergency phone numbers for fire, police, poison control, paramedics, your work number and the phone numbers for a neighbor or relative. Keep them in a handy spot and show the kids where to find them. Also, show children how to work the door and window locks.

Tell them to notice before they go inside whether the front or back door is ajar, whether a window is broken or whether a suspicious-looking person is nearby. That means they should not enter the house. They should hurry to a neighbor's home or a safe public phone and dial 911.

Stress that they must not open the door to strangers for any reason, or tell telephone callers that they're home alone.

Advice for Hiring Babysitters

Your babysitter has a big responsibility—the safety of your children. Be sure that your babysitter is prepared for emergency and has a good grounding in crime-proofing.

Some tips:

How to keep latch-key kids safe

Some tips for protecting children who are home alone after school:

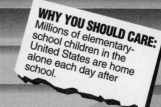
What children should watch for

If the door to the house is ajar, a window is broken or a suspicious-looking person is nearby. . .

- **DO NOT** go into the house.

- **DO** go quickly to a neighbor's house or public phone where people are nearby and call the police.

What children should know

 The **check-in procedure** to follow with a parent at work or with a neighbor.

 Emergency phone numbers for fire, police, poison control, paramedics, parent's workplace, a neighbor and a relative.

Not to open the door or let strangers into the house for any reason.

Not to tell telephone callers that they are home alone .

How to work the door and window locks.

SOURCES: National Crime Prevention Council, Bureau of Justice Statistics; research by PAT CARR

Interview all new babysitters. Ask for personal references—and check them.

Make sure the sitter knows how to reach you in case of emergency, as well as his or her own parent in case you can't be reached. Also jot a note with your home address in case the sitter needs to summon help.

Show the sitter where police, fire department and neighbors' phone numbers are posted in your home. Point out fire escape routes.

Give the sitter these instructions: lock the doors. Do not let strangers inside. Do not leave the kids by themselves—for any reason.

Let the sitter know if you're expecting any deliveries.

Make the sitter aware of any medical problems that might arise—and how to deal with them. Leave your family doctor's phone number in case of emergency.

School Crime

Kids spend more waking hours in school than anywhere else. Unfortunately, crime has moved into the schools with them, and it follows them onto the surrounding streets. One in eight students nationally has been afraid of being attacked on the way to or from school. About one of six children says gangs are at their school. And more than three-quarters of thefts and one-third of violent crimes against young teens happen at or around school, according to the U.S. Justice Department. What can you and your kids do?

Preventing crime can be as simple as designing schools to be more open architecturally to make it easier to spot troublemakers. Fort Lauderdale architect Donald Singer came up with a prototype of a safer school building, with big classroom windows so teachers can see into the yard and entrances that force kids to pass in front of the administration and guidance offices. The bottom line: safe-minded schools shut out the outside, so strangers can't wander around unnoticed, but open up on the inside so students and teachers won't feel closed in.

But parents and students can take measures to enhance safety from crime at any school, regardless of design or year of construction.

Parents: point out for your younger children safe spots along the way to school—a firehouse, a police station, a hospital, a library, stores or offices. Establish neighborhood "safe houses" where kids can go if they need help. If crime and disruption on school buses are a constant problem, parents can lobby their local school board to install closed-circuit TV cameras on each bus.

For kids, here are tips for keeping safe in and around school:

❑ Don't fight if another student demands your lunch money, homework, jewelry or anything else.

❑ If you see someone at school with a weapon, discreetly tell a teacher, an assistant principal, a school counselor or other school official. If you hear a rumor that someone at school has a weapon, tell someone in authority.

❑ Don't carry guns or weapons. Brass knuckles, razor knives and other sharp objects count as weapons. In many school districts, students who carry weapons are expelled on the spot.

❑ Stay on campus during school hours.

❑ Avoid walking to and from school alone. Map out a safe route to and from school, and do not take shortcuts, especially through dark or deserted areas.

❑ On buses, sit as close to the driver as you can.

How to stay safe at school

Some tips for helping children protect
themselves from theft and violence at school:

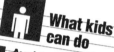

What kids can do

- **Avoid walking to and from school alone.** Don't stop anywhere on the way.

- **Stay on campus** during school hours.

- **Avoid wearing clothing associated with gangs.** Don't wear expensive jewelry.

- **Do not fight** with a student who demands your money or property. Comply, then report the incident to a school official.

What parents can do

- **Find the safest route** to and from school by walking the neighborhood with your child. Avoid danger spots such as alleys, wooded areas.

- **Create a school safe corridor** by volunteering to supervise walking routes to and from school.

- **Check out the school's policies** on absent children. Are parents called when a child is absent?

- **Help supervise the campus** during "passing periods" and patrol parking lots before and after school.

SOURCES: National School Safety Center, Long
Beach Press-Telegram; research by PAT CARR

About 270,000 guns are taken to school every day, according to a University of Michigan study. More than three million crimes are committed in or near 85,000 public schools by students.

❑ Don't wear expensive clothes, gold jewelry, leather coats and pricey sneakers—all the rage with punks. "We tell people to put their jewelry inside their clothing," says New York officer Merri Pearsall. "It makes sense not to wear things that are popular with criminals."

Parents and kids should insist school officials institute more crime-fighting measures. Many schools today use metal detectors to randomly screen students for weapons, either during the day or after-school events. They also conduct random searches of lockers and school grounds, sometimes using trained weapons-sniffing dogs. Others employ security guards or prohibit kids from leaving school grounds for lunch. In some communities, public school students wear uniforms to boost spirit and reduce crime.

How to Avoid Gangs and Gang Violence

Youth gangs are a problem in many communities, bringing with them fear and violence. Gang members vandalize property, paint walls with graffiti, threaten residents and business owners and intimidate other young people, according to the National Crime Prevention Council, which produces the brochure "Tools to Involve Parents in Gang Prevention." Call 202-466-6272 for a copy.

Parents who see gang members in their neighborhoods should call police. Paint over graffiti. If their presence is not challenged, gang members may view that as a sign of weakness and take over the neighborhood, says Patti Russell, a crime analyst for the Orange County sheriff's office in Orlando, Fla.

But kids may be far more likely to come into contact with gang members than older people. Parents should walk their children to and from school or wait with them at the bus stop. Here is advice on how kids can avoid gangs:

❏ Don't wear clothes that are the same color as gang clothes (say, red or blue, if those are gang colors in your school). If gangs wear all blue and you wear blue, you could be aligning yourself with them unwittingly.

❏ Don't approach individuals in cars who seem to want information—it could be a drive-by shooting setup.

❏ Don't hang around graffiti-marked walls; you're in gang territory. Don't hang out with gang members, or wannabe gang members. Don't take part in writing graffiti.

❏ Don't buy designer clothes whose initials may be confused for a gang name. For instance, the "BK" on British Knights sneakers could mean membership in the "Blood Killer" gang of Los Angeles. If a member of a rival gang sees you, you may be harassed.

❏ Get involved in sports, clubs and extracurricular activities so that gangs won't pressure you to join. If they try to pressure you, don't act scared. Try not to go anywhere alone. Stick with family and friends. Avoid trouble spots where drugs are sold, or where gangs hang out.

❏ If someone harasses you, talk to parents, school officials and police. If a gang member pushes you, don't automatically push back. Try to talk yourself out of the situation. Stand up for yourself and be strong. If you get into a fight, talk to an adult afterward.

❏ Don't go into unfamiliar neighborhoods that could be

gang territory. In some cities, if you're wearing red in a "Crip" neighborhood, you could be mistaken for a member of a rival gang and be harmed. If you're wearing blue in a "Blood" gang neighborhood, the same could happen.

Spotting Gang Signs

Not every teen who sports a tattoo or wears baggy pants is in a gang, but police say kids and parents should still pay attention to these signs of possible gang membership:

❑ Tattoos: Many gang members tattoo the initials of their gang and their gang moniker on their stomach, arms, back, neck or forehead. Tattoos, however, could indicate past gang membership, not present.

❑ Clothing: Some items that may be associated with gangs include wearing baseball caps in a certain position, hair nets, bandanas, cut-off baggy pants with white knee socks, pants worn very low to the hips, special shoelace colors, and black military-style web belts with buckles displaying gang initials. However, be aware that styles change.

❑ Graffiti: Most gang members have address books or wallets with their tags or gang names and other gang graffiti written on them.

❑ Hand signals: When rival gang members encounter each other, they challenge one another by throwing signs.

❑ Slogans and jargon: Gangs have their own language, words with specific meaning to fellow gang members.

Preventing Sexual Assault

Sexual assault happens to many girls and boys, and in fact rape occurs more commonly to minors than to adults, according to a recent study by the National Victim Center. "The youthfulness of our victims is a shame," says Anne Seymour, one of the authors of the report.

How to prevent these devastating experiences? The answer is education.

Children still can be overpowered both mentally and physically by an attacker, but education can improve the odds that young victims will be able to cope with the attack. Education also makes it more likely the child will report the aggressor, who is usually a relative or a familiar person, says Susan Osborne, community organizer for the Minnesota Coalition for Sexual Assault, an umbrella organization of 36 rape counseling centers.

Most kids are secretive about sexually abusive behavior, so it's up to parents and teachers to spot suspicious signs. Watch for children engaging in activity beyond their age development, such as a 3-year-old engaging in oral sexual activity, says Joyce Wright, communications director for HAVEN, a Pontiac, Mich., agency that helps families in crisis. Explore comments that seem questionable, such as: "Jimmy kisses me funny."

Teach children the following tips:

The National Victim Center surveyed 4,008 adult women, many of whom said that during their youth, someone forced them to have intercourse, oral or anal sex, or inserted something inside them. Three out of four rape victims knew their attacker: 29 percent said they were attacked by neighbors or other familiar non-relatives, 16 percent by other relatives, 11 percent by a father or stepfather, 10 percent by a boyfriend or ex-boyfriend, 9 percent by a husband or ex-husband, 22 percent by a stranger and 3 percent by someone they couldn't or wouldn't identify.

Some touches are good; some are bad. "Bad touches" can scare, confuse or hurt a child. If anyone touches a child in a way he or she doesn't like or understand, the child should say, "No. Get away!" Tell him or her to talk to a trusted adult. Children have a right to their own bodies and feelings. They have the right not to be touched inappropriately on private parts.

Tell kids who they can turn to for help—family members, school personnel, etc.

Tell them to trust their senses. For example, say: "If your feelings tell you something is not OK, talk to a trusted adult. Keep telling various trusted adults until someone believes you and takes action. It's never too late to tell."

Sexual assault and rape happen to many girls and boys, and in fact rape occurs more commonly to minors than to adults, according to a study by the National Victim Center. More than six out of 10 of all rape cases occurred before the victims reached the age of 18. Twenty-nine percent of all forcible rapes in America occur when the victim was less than 11 years old.

Missing Children/Kidnapping

Abducted kids usually are taken by family members—not strangers. It's at least 10,000 times more likely that family members are to blame when children are missing. About 350,000 children are abducted every year by family members, often by the frustrated parent who lost a bitter custody fight, according to a study ordered by Congress. Only 200 to 300 children a year are taken by strangers.

Child Find of America, a nonprofit organization started by a mother searching for her missing child, has compiled a profile of potential abductors, including parental abductors: They're typically impulsive, hostile, revengeful or abusive, with a poor job record. And they usually know how to support themselves while moving from town to town without detection (or someone is willing to support them financially).

The organization suggests these prevention tips:

Make sure your child knows how to write down his or her name, address and phone number with area code. Using a map of the United States, have your youngster color in the correct home state and identify it.

Show the kids how a telephone works. Explain what an area code means. Teach the child to call Child Find at 1-800-I-AM-LOST in case he or she is lost someday and has forgotten the home phone number (but knows his or her name, address and state).

Teach your child to keep you in sight at all times and not to wander off. Always know where your child is, and establish strict procedures for picking up the youngster at school, after a movie or other places.

Tell your child never to go anywhere with anyone who doesn't know a frequently changed family code word—such as "banana," as discussed earlier. If someone tries to pick up the child, he or she could say, "What is the code word?" If the grown-up doesn't know the word, the child should not go with that person.

Teach your child about abduction in a calm way, similar to teaching any other important coping skill.

Listen closely if your child talks about someone he or she met while you were gone.

Take head-and-shoulders photos every six months for children 6 and younger, or yearly for older kids. Note their birthmarks and distinguishing features. Ask your police department how you can get your children fingerprinted.

Never leave kids unattended. It can take an abductor less than a minute to run off with your child. When youngsters reach an age where parents don't need to watch them constantly, join or establish a block parent program. A parent screened by local police could run a "safe house" bearing a clear symbol that kids are taught to recognize. More informally, tell your child which trusted neighbor's home is safe.

Tell your youngster what to do if someone is following him or her: If it's a car, turn around and go the other way. If the car turns around, too, hurry into a nearby store, government office or other safe place and tell an employee. Tell the employee to call police.

If you and the child's other parent are separated or divorced, get legal custody of your child. If you think the child may be removed from the country, get the youngster a passport. Tell the passport office that your child must not be taken out of the country without your permission.

You can lessen the odds that the other parent will run off with your child. Don't hold out on visitation times with your child. Try to be civil.

Keep important information about the other parent that may help track him or her down if the child disappears—Social Security number, driver's license number, or a list of relatives and friends.

If the unthinkable happens and your child is long overdue at home, call family members and friends who might know where your child is. Then call police. They will type your child's name into a nationwide computer system for missing children. Give a fingerprint card and a recent photo to police investigators. Child Find of America (1-800-I-AM-LOST) helps find missing children.

Call your local newspaper, TV and radio stations to get your child's story and photo before the public. Child Find suggests printing posters with your child's photo, description and contact phone numbers and distributing them around the area.

If you think the child's other parent abducted your child, get a felony warrant for his or her arrest (as long as you have legal custody of the child).

The FBI has these additional suggestions:

❏ Make sure outside doors, windows and screens are securely locked before going to sleep. Keep the door to the children's rooms open so you can hear unusual noises.

❏ Be sure the child's room isn't readily accessible from the outside.

❏ Keep the home well-lighted if it is necessary to leave children alone at home. Avoid obvious indications that you're not home and that the kids may be inside unprotected. Don't leave garage doors open or newspapers left outside the house.

❏ Instruct babysitters and housekeepers not to let strangers in the house.

❏ Don't advertise family finances or routines. Kidnappers frequently have their victims under surveillance for several days before an abduction so they may acquaint themselves with the family's habits.

If Your Child Is Kidnapped by a Stranger

If your child has been kidnapped by a stranger, look in the front of the phone directory for the number of the FBI,

---

Teens are more victimized by crime than all other age groups, including adults. One in four thefts and three in 10 violent crimes happen to teens, according to the U.S. Department of Justice.

---

and call. The emergency number at FBI headquarters is 202-
324-3000.

Don't tell anyone about the kidnapping or ransom demands except for the immediate family or investigating officers. Turn over letters demanding payment of ransom to
officers as soon as possible. Don't handle the matter yourself. Don't touch or disturb anything at the scene of the
crime. Tiny particles of evidence invisible to the naked eye
could be destroyed.

Most of all, be calm. Try to keep up a normal routine
around the home and at work. Help officers as much as possible: give them photos, describe your missing child in de-
tail and don't leave out his or her personal habits. The FBI's
goal is simple: a safe return of your child.

Halloween Safety

When your kids go out to trick or treat, go with them. Or make
sure they walk in groups with an adult escort who is carrying a
flashlight. Stay in your own neighborhood and/or go only to homes
that you know. In some communities, local merchants sponsor
trick-or-treat outings. Caution kids to accept wrapped treats only.
Tell them not to eat any treats until parents have checked them.
Some hospitals offer free X-rays of trick-or-treat items.

5

Crime-Proofing in Special Situations

Women and children are not the only groups singled out by criminals. Senior citizens and the disabled may be targeted because their physical abilities are limited; college students often fall victim to crime because young people are casual about their belongings and their safety. Travelers also tend to be casual or overconfident in new environments. The most basic advice for everyone in these groups: stay alert and be aware of your surroundings.

College Students

College is the time of your life when a young person is supposed to be broadening his or her horizons. Thinking about crime doesn't come to mind, nor does crime figure prominently in glossy college brochures.

But college crime exists: some 21,478 burglaries, 7,350 car thefts, 3,224 aggravated assaults, 1,353 robberies and 17 murders occurred at 774 campuses in 1993, according to the *Chronicle of Higher Education.*

Connie and Howard Clery, whose daughter was killed during a robbery of her dorm room at Pennsylvania's Lehigh University in 1986, suggest that parents and students ask about more than academics or scholarships when visiting a prospective college. How many felonies were committed on campus during the past three years? How many rapes, robberies, assaults, burglaries and homicides? What is the ratio of students to campus police and security officers?

Thanks to lobbying by the Clerys, all colleges and universities whose students receive financial aid are legally required to compile annual statistics on reported crimes on campus for a federal crime report. Of course, these don't include petty thefts like stealing a hot plate.

And when comparing campuses, remember to compare apples and oranges. The figures aren't adjusted to account for the number of students. A huge university with 100 crimes may turn out to fare better statistically than a tiny college with 10 reported crimes.

Security on Campus offers a crime questionnaire you can send along with college applications for administrators to fill out and return to you. Send a self-addressed, stamped envelope to: Security on Campus, 215 W. Church Road, Suite 200, King of Prussia, PA 19406. The federal Student Right to Know and Campus Security Act, passed in 1990, requires colleges to answer an applicant's request for these statistics.

Realize that not all crimes are reported. Only about one in 10 campus rape victims reports the crime, according to Security on Campus.

You can do your own sleuthing, too. Walk around the campus library, student center and other buildings at night—when many students trek back to their dorm rooms. See any questionable walkways or dark parking lots? Are emergency phones, commuter buses or escort services available? Read the campus newspaper, which probably will be more frank about crime than school administrators, for stories revealing potential problems. Talk to the school's director of public safety to find out more about crime and steps taken to keep the campus safe. Ask whether victims can get medical or psychological help. Go to your local library to read the *Chronicle of Higher Education*'s reports on individual colleges and crimes reported on campus.

Find out whether residence halls have security monitors around the clock, and whether these monitors are trained professionals. Check whether dorm doors lock automatically or have electronic arms that warn when doors are propped open (a common occurrence on campus). Ask whether underage state liquor laws are enforced by campus police.

Some schools are taking the initiative in battling crime. They are educating students as early as the first week on campus—during campus orientation—on how to keep from becoming targets. Rutgers University in New Jersey has a Street Smart Survival program, in which students act out mock crimes so they'll know how to handle the real thing if it should occur.

What students need to remember is that basic crime-proofing techniques outlined in this book work on campus, too. Students should keep doors locked, and not allow anyone into their dorm who doesn't belong. They should use a campus escort at night, if available, if the only option is walking alone.

Drinking is part of college life on many campuses, but it can fuel crime. Alcohol plays a role in as many as nine out of 10 violent crimes, according to the Campus Violence Prevention Center at Towson State University in Maryland.

Some schools, such as the University of Texas at Austin, offer cabs to pick up inebriated students anywhere in town on weekends to take them home—for free.

Other tips, from the Towson State University Campus Violence Prevention Center and other experts:

❏ Report malfunctioning locks to dorm officials.

❏ If you see a stranger in your dorm, you have a right to question him or her. Ask, "May I help you?" This lets the stranger know you've noticed him or her and could discourage criminal activity.

❏ Don't pick up a drifter or another stranger and bring him onto campus. One campus security officer calls them "Trojan horses." Well-meaning students sometimes feel sorry for vagrants and offer them a meal and a bath back at the dorm, but such kindness could spell trouble. In one case, a drifter did not harm his benefactor, but attacked and killed another student.

❏ Many crimes against college students start with casual conversation. If you're overly friendly, you may be seen as an easy target. Trust your gut reaction: if you feel uneasy, leave.

❏ Look alert when walking. Criminals look for people who are depressed, distracted, discouraged, lost.

❏ Find out more about new acquaintances before offering too much information about yourself. You'll be meeting many new people and will long to attain close friendships. But take time to get to know people.

❏ Beware of strangers who may tell you a story to get you away from a crowd. People pretending to have broken legs have taken advantage of kind and unsuspecting students. Another ploy is to say you must hurry to help someone who's injured.

❏ College students are at greater risk of sexual assault than others. It is estimated that as many as one in four

For a crime questionnaire you can send along with college applications, send a self-addressed, stamped envelope to: Security on Campus, 215 W. Church Road, Suite 200, King of Prussia, PA 19406.

American college and university women will become victims of sexual attack by the time they graduate. For more information, see the section on date rape in Chapter 3.

College Student Safety Tips

Some tips for college students:

❑ Make sure your locks were changed before you move in.

❑ Have a deadbolt lock on your dorm room. Keep doors locked.

❑ Make sure your air conditioner is secured (not merely sitting in a window) so a thief can't remove it from the outside.

❑ Have a plan of escape in case of emergency.

❑ Let your roommate or a friend know where you're going, with whom, and when you will be back.

❑ Report suspicious persons or activity.

❑ Let friends and dates know what you consider appropriate behavior. Trust your instincts. If a situation does not feel right, get away.

❑ Walk alertly, confidently, and keep to well-lighted, well-traveled areas.

❑ Look for suspicious people before leaving a building.

❑ As you approach your car, have keys in hand and look underneath the car for potential attackers.

❑ Keep your car locked at all times, especially when you are in it.

❏ Keep a "Call Police" emergency banner in your car.

❏ Check for loiterers before leaving your car.

Travelers

Safety while on vacation or on a business trip is simple: just be sensible. "There are no statistics that tell us traveling is unsafe," says Jean O'Neil of the National Crime Prevention Council. But "not using your common sense is unsafe—no matter where you are."

Some tips from the American Hotel & Motel Association:

❏ Check to see that windows and connecting room doors are locked.

❏ Don't answer the door in a hotel or motel room without verifying who it is. If a person claims to be an employee, call the front desk.

❏ Close the door securely whenever you are in your room. Use all the locks.

❏ Don't display your guest room keys in public, or leave them in places where they can be easily stolen.

❏ Do not draw attention to yourself by displaying cash or expensive jewelry.

❏ Don't invite strangers to your room.

❏ Don't leave valuables in your car. Have the hotel or motel lock up valuables in a safe deposit box.

❏ When returning to your hotel or motel late in the evening, use the main entrance of the hotel. Be observant and look around before entering parking lots.

Security-conscious hotels have guest rooms with deadbolt locks that cannot be opened from the outside with guest or master keys, and a lock that automatically engages when the door closes. They also have peepholes.

Many hotels and motels have installed keyless locking systems, usually a card with no printed room number. Growing numbers of hoteliers also require that their front desk staff refrain from announcing room numbers during check-in.

Outside the hotel, keep your wits about you.

"Very often, victims set themselves up," says Thomas Seamon, Philadelphia's deputy police commissioner for operations. "Don't stand there with a camera around your neck and your mouth gaping open. Pay attention to your surroundings. If you want to read a map, go into a restaurant or coffee shop; don't stand on the corner doing it. It's a dead giveaway that you're new in town and you don't know where you are or what you're doing. People who look like tourists are targets."

Be cautious when seated in an outdoor café.

If you're driving and you get lost, don't pull over on the side of the road just anywhere. Drive to a well-lighted public place that looks safe.

If you suspect you're being followed, drive to a public area with good lighting and preferably other people. Then call the police.

Beware of people who yell, honk and point at your car as if something were wrong. Also, ignore those who motion and ask you to stop and lend help, bump your vehicle from behind, or flash lights at you. (See Chapter 6 for more information.)

Don't pick up hitchhikers. Don't go into an alley with someone selling cheap watches or marijuana. Don't leave with strangers you've met in bars.

"You're on vacation, but the crooks are not," says Maj. Jerry Brown, commander of the Honolulu police department's Waikiki division.

Be aware that a long airplane flight, jet lag, sleep deprivation and a strange environment can disorient you and make it more likely you'll be victimized.

Make sure your hotel is in a reputable neighborhood, particularly if you're traveling alone. When you go out, let someone know your plans so you will be missed if something happens.

When traveling on business, keep a list of emergency phone numbers of people in your home office so you can reach them after hours. Share your itinerary with key people, but don't make it widely known.

The biggest problem among business travelers is complacency and a macho attitude, says Robert R. Burke, director of corporate security for Monsanto Co. "Travelers tend to believe that they are invulnerable or invisible when visiting a strange city," he says. "Therefore, they do things they would not do in their hometowns."

When Traveling Overseas

Going overseas demands more preparation than making sure your passport is current. You need to be prepared if you encounter anti-American attitudes or high levels of crime against tourists. Begin by finding out as much as possible about the political and social conditions of the country you plan to visit. The State Department has information that is constantly updated.

Dress conservatively. Don't send a "wealthy American executive" message to a criminal or terrorist. Leave behind cowboy hats, baseball caps, T-shirts and other blatantly American clothing.

Make sure your passport doesn't expire before or during

How to keep your luggage safe

Some tips for protecting your luggage while traveling:

WHY YOU SHOULD CARE: About 10,000 bags do not arrive at their intended destination each day; 100 are irretrievably lost or stolen.

Flight tags
Remove all old flight tags to prevent your luggage from being sent to the wrong destination.

DTW

Luggage straps
Put a strap or tie around each suitcase or a seal on the zipper to provide an extra barrier to thieves.

Valuables
Never store valuables in your luggage; locks can be easily opened in transit by baggage handlers.

Advice on IDs

- Put identification tags on the outside and inside of your suitcases.

- Use a business card for an ID or, if you don't have a business address, use just your phone number for identification. Using your home address is an advertisement for would-be thieves, who could head to your home knowing you're not there.

SOURCES: Federal Bureau of Investigation 1992 Uniform Crime Reports, Citizen's Crime Watch, Air Transport Association.

your trip. Bring extra photos in case you need them for visas or if you lose your passport.

In cities where purse snatching and pickpockets are common, carry a photocopy of the first page of your passport. Keep the passport protected in the hotel's safety deposit box or a safe in your room.

In underdeveloped nations, always have an escort who is a native. Check his or her references.

Know how to use public phones. In some countries, you need to buy a special card; others require coins.

Learn key phrases in the native language so you can communicate in an emergency. Things like: I need help. Call the police. I have been injured. Where is the police station?

Know the location of the nearest U.S. consulate or embassy. As a U.S. citizen, you can seek help if you lose your passport or have an emergency.

The Disabled

As the world becomes more sensitive and accommodating to the disabled, they can enjoy more of what life has to offer. Unfortunately, crime is also included in the offer.

Some tips from police officer Tobie Cozy of Fulton, Ohio, who launched a crime-prevention program for people with physical challenges:

❑ Don't advertise your disability on a license plate. Get a disability card that can be removed from the window at any time so robbers aren't alerted that you're a potential target.

❑ Motorists who use wheelchairs should leave plenty of space in parking lots to get in and out of their vehicles. If you feel threatened, leave your wheelchair outside the vehicle—and pull yourself inside.

❏ When at a restaurant, movie or other public place, try to park your wheelchair with its back to the wall to keep people from sneaking up behind you.

❏ If possible, install a wheelchair ramp inside your garage, not outside your home, to avoid advertising the fact that you're disabled.

❏ Vary your activities and routine so you're not an easy mark for criminals.

❏ Tell family and friends where you're going and when you expect to return.

❏ Travel with someone you know.

❏ Carry only as much money as you'll need. Never display a lot of cash.

❏ Know your neighbors. Know whom you can trust in case of emergency.

❏ When taking public transportation, sit near the driver. Try to appear assertive even when in an unfamiliar setting.

Senior Citizens

Older people are victims of crime less often than other age groups. That's right—less often. The bad news is that they're likely to suffer more—mentally, physically and economically—if they are attacked by a criminal.

Still, don't be overly alarmed.

"Often, fear of crime is an even bigger problem than crime itself," says Mary Lindemann of Michigan's state office of services for the aging. "Elders shut themselves in. Because they are afraid, they don't go out, and they are victimized less as a result, but their quality of life suffers."

Older people make good targets for criminals for several reasons: seniors often follow regular routines, they are more vulnerable physically and they often are reluctant to prosecute.

Regardless of how old you are, the following steps can help you avoid being victimized at home or on the street:

If someone you don't know comes to the door to use the phone, never let him or her inside. Get the number through the closed door and make the call for the person.

Be suspicious of any stranger who says he or she will share a wad of cash found in the street, a lottery prize or other money with you. Think: would you share money with a total stranger?

Ask police crime-prevention officers how you can mark your valuables with easily identifiable numbers, such as driver's license numbers.

Keep your money and securities in a bank—not under the mattress, where a thief will think to look.

If you're planning to go on a walk, consider doing it with a friend, or walk confidently and on a direct route. Purse snatchers have become a bit more violent. "They used to run, snatch the purse and keep running," says social worker Magali Amador, of Jewish Family Service of Greater Miami. "Now, they run and snatch their purses, then push people to the ground and kick them, too."

To discourage purse snatchers, carry a small coin purse, not a large bag, and keep it in a pocket. If another bag is needed, carry a clutch purse tucked under an arm. Clutch purses are harder to steal than large bags. Avoid wearing a bag that attaches around the waist—a thief could cut it off or pull hard, causing you to fall. Don't carry large amounts of cash. Leave your checkbook at home; carry only one or two blank checks with you. Remain calm if your purse is snatched. Throw the purse away from you and sit down. Try to get a look at the thief to provide a good description to police. (See graphic on "How to Describe a Criminal" in Chapter 2.)

Use direct deposit for Social Security and pension checks to avoid thefts from the mailbox.

Consider owning a dog, even a small one, to give you both protection and companionship. A leashed dog accompanying you on a walk also can give a thief second thoughts.

Keep doors and windows locked. Criminals don't have to break in to do the job—doors and windows are left unlocked in about half of all crimes, says one crime-prevention expert. Turn on the lights when you get up at night. If the house is being watched, a burglar will avoid a home where the residents are awake.

Use a double lock on sliding glass doors, and latch bar or lock on windows. If you don't have deadbolt locks on outside doors, then have them installed. Consider installing a peephole to identify a visitor at the front door. Can't afford these things? Crime victims on fixed incomes may qualify for free security devices such as window bars and better locks. Ask a social worker in a local or state office of aging whether programs are available in your area.

Devise an informal signal with neighbors so they know you're OK—maybe raise a certain window blind or turn on a particular light.

When away, leave on a light and TV (or the radio tuned to a talk show). Burglars usually target homes where no one is home or where a woman lives alone.

Let a good neighbor know your vacation plans. Have neighbors pick up the mail, or tell your postal carrier to stop delivery. Stop newspaper delivery and arrange to have someone mow the lawn. Ask a neighbor to park a car in your driveway to make it appear someone is home. Tell neighbors to call police if they see anything suspicious. (For more information, see Chapter 1.)

Consider taking a class to learn more ways to protect yourself so you'll feel freer to take walks and travel. The Miramar Civic Center in Miramar, Fla., for instance, teaches seniors to ward off muggers and con artists.

Check to see if your community offers special crime prevention services to senior citizens. In Fulton, Ohio, for example, police officers have "adopted" senior citizens who live alone and see if anything is needed. Call your local police, the elderly affairs office of your state or local government or the United Way to find out about a program near you.

Senior facts:

☛ Surveys show the number of crimes committed against older people is no greater than against other age groups, but the level of fear is much greater. So is the sense of loss.

☛ Mature travelers are no greater targets of thieves, pickpockets and other criminals than younger tourists. They're simply more concerned about security because they've had more years to understand the consequences of crime.

☛ Older people are almost twice as likely as others to be seriously injured and require hospitalization following a criminal act.

6

Crime-Proofing Your Car

Cars are safety havens for most of us, an extension of our homes. We spend so much time in our cars, enveloped in relative privacy while enjoying the freedom of the open road, that we are shocked when crime confronts us at the wheel. Yet more and more Americans are experiencing that shock.

Most common crimes: auto theft, and theft of valuables and accessories from a motor vehicle. A car is stolen every 20 seconds, according to the FBI's "crime clock" for 1992. The average value of goods stolen from cars that year was $555.

But we also are conscious of our vulnerability on the roadside. Abductions, random attacks on stranded drivers, carjackings—these kinds of less-common crimes alarm both police and the motoring public.

The old rules of the road—heeding all traffic lights, stopping for accidents, pulling over for a nap—need to be reevaluated these days. "Years ago, they'd tell you to pull over and take 40 winks if you were tired," says Harvey Baxter, a county judge in Miami. "I won't do that anymore."

Each situation has to be judged on its merits, but police and judges may be lenient toward drivers who bend traffic rules when they fear for their safety.

Here are some steps you can take to protect yourself and your car.

On the road. A breakdown on the road leaves you vulnerable to criminals. Keep your car in good running order. That means checking for loose wires, keeping your spare tire inflated and making sure all mechanical systems are OK. Join an auto club that provides towing service and emergency roadside mechanical assistance. Consider buying a cellular phone or CB radio so you can call for help if you need it. This advice is especially meaningful if you travel alone, at night or in high-crime areas.

This seems so basic that it shouldn't need mention, but how many of us ride around with the fuel tank needle on "empty"? Make sure you have enough gasoline to get to your destination.

If your car breaks down on the road, get out and raise the hood and get back inside. Turn on the emergency flashers. The switch is usually on the steering column. Practice turning it on and off so you won't have to hunt through your instruction manual in an emergency.

Lock the doors and raise windows. You can also tie a white cloth to the antenna or door handle. If you have an emergency banner, place it in the windshield. Emergency banners that say "Call Police" or "Get Help" are widely sold in drug stores and auto supply shops.

If you've had a flat tire, assess your situation. Decide whether it's safe to change a tire. If it's not, consider driving slowly on the shoulder until you get to an exit or to a well-lighted business. Yes, you'll ruin the tire or the rim, but that may be wiser than being stranded on the roadside.

How to safeguard your car

Some tips for protecting your car from thieves and yourself from assault or robbery while you're driving:

What to do if your vehicle breaks down

- Raise the hood or tie a white cloth to the street-side door handle.
- Stay in car with doors locked.
- If someone stops, ask them to phone for assistance.
- Consider installing a CB radio or cellular phone.

WHY YOU SHOULD CARE: In 1991, motor vehicle thefts cost victims about $8.5 billion.

Parking safety

- Always lock your car and take the keys with you.
- Avoid parking in isolated areas.
- Be especially alert in unstaffed lots and enclosed garages.
- If you must leave a key with a parking attendant, leave only the ignition key.

Good maintenance

- Keep your car in good running condition.
- Make sure the car has enough gas.

Keys and paper work

- Keep the keys to your home and car separate.
- Keep your tag and vehicle identification numbers with your driver's license.
- Keep the registration with you, not in the car.

Avoiding trouble

- If you think someone is following you, drive to the nearest police or fire station, open service station or other open business.
- Never pick up hitchhikers. Never hitchhike.

SOURCES: National Crime Prevention Council, Bureau of Justice Statistics; research by PAT CARR

Be cautious about accepting help from good Samaritans. If someone stops, crack your window and ask him or her to get help or to call a tow truck. Hand your rescuer a quarter to make the call.

Never get into a stranger's car. And don't pick up hitchhikers.

If confronted by someone who is armed, your first thought must be for your own safety, not for your vehicle. Hand over the car keys; scream or create another diversion if doing so will enable you to get away safely.

Resist if a stranger attempts to force you into his vehicle. Why? Once you're in his car, he has two options for getting rid of you: hurt you, or set you free and run the risk of your being a witness against him. (See Chapter 2 for more detailed information on protecting yourself in a confrontation.)

Parking lots. Another place where you are in danger is the parking lot. People have been abducted or attacked in parking lots, especially at shopping malls or in large commercial parking garages. Elevators and stairwells are trouble spots. In response, managers of parking garages and commercial properties have become much more sensitive to security, increasing patrols and issuing safety brochures to customers. Some have installed sophisticated crime-fighting devices, including panic buttons, closed-circuit television and voice-activated monitors that can speed help to your side. But high-tech equipment can't do it all.

Have your car keys in your hand—not in your pocket, not at the bottom of your purse. You'll be able to enter your car quickly instead of fumbling around while someone sneaks up on you.

Keep aware of your surroundings and of suspicious people loitering in the lot. Try to walk with other people and park close to your destination. Ask for an escort from the mall or office security department if you leave after dark or if you're concerned.

Generally, open lots are safer than enclosed garages. In either, choose a spot as close as possible to the cashier. In a garage, try to stay on the ground floor, and be careful on elevators and in stairwells.

If you park your car to read a map or eat lunch, choose a busy, well-lighted spot. Someone could approach you while you're distracted, so be watchful. "These people are looking for drivers who look lost or distracted or confused," says Ray Lang, a spokesman for Miami Police. "You have to be aware of your surroundings. You have to know where you're going, and you need to be looking around, watching for situations that don't look right."

On expressway off-ramps and street corners. In some areas, roadside robbers wait for you to stop at traffic lights or on backed-up expressway ramps. They throw a rock or porcelain spark plug at your window, shattering the glass. Sometimes they keep a brick wrapped in a paper bag for the same purpose. Then they take your purse or briefcase.

Look out for loiterers on a street corner. Someone sitting on top of a bus bench may actually be trying to see inside your car, looking for purses or briefcases within easy reach. Keep your valuables out of sight or locked in the trunk.

To protect yourself, be sure to leave yourself maneuvering room—a car's length away from other cars.

Some drivers treat their windows with safety film. The film does not make your windows unbreakable, but it takes three or four hard blows before the window shatters, potentially giving you time to drive away. The film also can protect you from being cut by flying glass.

Robbers especially prey on women driving alone, the elderly, people driving new or expensive cars, people wearing flashy jewelry and drivers who look lost. Try not to read a map on a street corner; pull into a restaurant to read it inside or go to a safe-looking gasoline station for directions.

If you approach a red light and feel threatened, consider clearing yourself of traffic and going through the red light. It's not legal, but most police officers will understand if you explain.

Keep a whistle on your key chain. It may startle your assailant or draw attention to your situation. You can also honk your horn or set off your car alarm.

In your driveway. Check your rearview mirror as you approach your house. Robbers can follow your car, wait for you to pull into your driveway and rush you as your feet hit the pavement. Their goal: your purse or your wallet, your jewelry, your car keys, even the keys to your house. "They generally have a car," says Lt. Dick Masten, of the Miami Shores, Fla., police department. "One drives. One looks out. And one snatches. It's quick and it's easy."

These confrontations also can be deadly. Some people have been hurt on their own front lawns trying to defend themselves in such a confrontation.

The advice for preventing driveway crime is similar to that for preventing purse snatching: basically, leave valuables at home; carry little cash; don't wear attention-drawing jewelry. Park in well-lighted areas and always carry your car keys in your hand as you approach your car.

If you use an automatic garage door opener, be sure you don't admit a criminal into your garage when you open the door.

"If you're driving someone home, make sure they get safely in their house, and that they call you to make sure you got home OK," says Joan McKenna, president and founder of Women Against Rape, a group in Collingswood, Pa. "If you feel you're being followed, make a couple of turns, and if you still are, don't ever get out of your car. Drive to the nearest police station or gas station."

Tips away from home:

❑ Don't get out of your car until you're sure the area is free of suspicious strangers.

❑ Always keep an eye out for people who may be watching or following you.

If someone is following you:

❑ Don't go home. Go to the nearest police department or other safe well-lighted location. If you go home, you're giving away your address.

❑ Give police a description of the person and the vehicle. Take note of the color, make, model, year and condition of

---

If You Have Car Trouble

Don't panic:

☛ Turn on your emergency flashers.

☛ Raise the hood.

☛ Call for help on a cellular phone or CB radio, if you have one.

☛ Consider buying a cardboard dashboard sign that says "Call Police." Place it in the rear window. Or tie a white cloth to your antenna.

☛ Keep your windows up and the doors locked as you wait inside your car for help.

☛ If a stranger stops to help, ask him or her to call the police or a nearby garage. Do not take a ride with a stranger.

☛ Honk your horn or scream. If you have a car alarm, set it off. Blink your headlights. Blow a whistle. The idea is to catch someone's attention.

☛ If the assailant has a weapon, give up your car immediately.

☛ Get a description of the robber and the getaway car. Details to note: the license plate number; color, make, model, year and condition of the car; hair color, height, weight, clothing, scars, tattoos, accents and other distinguishing characteristics.

☛ Call the police as soon as the assailant leaves. If you aren't able to call, ask a witness or bystander to call 911.

☛ If your car was stolen, report it to the police right away. Have ready the make, model, year, color, license tag number, vehicle identification number and car tracking system number, if you have one. Report the theft to your insurance company.

the car. Get the license plate number if you can. To describe the person, try to notice hair color, height, scars, tattoos, accents and other distinguishing characteristics, such as gender, race and age.

Cellular Phones

While cellular phones don't deter crime, they are a useful safety device because they allow you to call for help or report a crime, says Capt. Bob Henderson, of the Rock Hill, N.C., police department.

Cellular phone prices and monthly service rates have dropped dramatically in recent years. Today, more than 12 million Americans have cellular phones.

Some tips:

❏ Dial 911 or your cellular carrier's emergency number if your car breaks down, if you witness an accident or crime or you see someone in distress on the road. In most cases, the call is free.

❏ Don't talk on the phone and write while you're driving. If you see a crime in progress or another emergency, try to find a safe place to pull over before calling or writing anything down. Many accidents are caused by people talking on their car phones.

❏ Program your phone for emergency numbers so you can speed-dial.

❏ Learn to operate your phone without looking at it.

❏ If your phone is permanently installed in your car, get a hands-free speaker so you won't have to hold the handset while talking. (Remember to remove the fuse or phone cable wire attached to the car battery before attempting to jump-start the car.)

❏ Prevent your cellular phone from being stolen. Try to park in a well-lighted area to deter thieves. Remove a portable phone when leaving your car.

Car Theft

We all pay for stolen cars. Stolen automobiles mean higher insurance rates and police attention diverted from other crimes.

America's stolen cars, at an average value of $4,700 each, were together worth more than $7.6 billion in 1992. Some 1.6 million motor vehicles were reported stolen that year, comprising about 13 percent of all property crimes.

Auto theft is largely a big-city problem, according to the FBI. For every 100,000 residents of cities with populations over 250,000, the 1992 motor vehicle theft rate was 1,591. In the nation's smallest cities (those with fewer than 10,000 residents), the rate was 246 and in rural counties, it was 117.

What kinds of cars do thieves look for? General Motors cars have been vulnerable because their parts are in demand and are valuable for resale. Favorite targets of most car thieves nationwide are Oldsmobile Cutlasses, Chevrolet Camaros and Buick Regals around 10 years old—not expensive luxury autos.

Cars are stolen from parking lots, university campuses, city streets and shopping centers. "The big malls are the big magnets," says Les Cravens, a detective with Metro-Dade County, Fla., police. "It's like going to a used car lot for

---

The Most Frequently Stolen Cars

Here are the car models most frequently stolen in the United States in 1993, according to CCC Information Services of Chicago.

1. 1984 Cutlass Supreme
2. 1986 Chevrolet Camaro
3. 1986 Cutlass
4. 1987 Cutlass
5. 1985 Cutlass
6. 1987 Camaro
7. 1984 Buick Regal
8. 1987 Chevrolet Caprice
9. 1991 Chevrolet T10 Blazer
10. 1985 Buick Regal

SOURCE: The Associated Press

---

some of these thieves." Even so, one-fourth of cars stolen in Florida are taken from the owner's driveway or garage.

Many car thieves are kids looking for a thrill or a joyride; some are criminals who need getaway cars. Others are professionals who sell stolen vehicles to "chop shops," which take the cars apart and sell them piecemeal to customers around the country and abroad. It's lucrative: One thief offered to sell a $35,000 Porsche engine for $10,000.

Another market for stolen cars is the export business. Thieves provide stolen cars for shipment to foreign countries, where they are sold for as much as three times their U.S. value.

Snapping open the steering column and hot-wiring the car is one of the most common methods used by car thieves. However, some thieves have opted for the "carjacking" method. (For more information, see the following pages.)

Tips for Avoiding Auto Theft

❏ If you have a home garage, keep your car inside it. Don't park on the street unless you have nowhere else to park.

❏ When you park your car, always roll up your windows and lock the doors, even in your driveway at home or your garage.

❏ Never leave your car, even for a few moments, with the keys in the ignition. A Gallup poll for the National Insurance Crime Bureau found that 14 percent of those surveyed said they did not always take the keys out of the ignition.

❏ Never leave your car—not even for a minute—when children are inside. Car thieves have inadvertently abducted children sleeping in their car seats while Mom or Dad ran into the store for a quick errand. Usually, the thieves abandon the car and the child. But don't take that chance.

❏ Don't hide a spare key anywhere on the car.

❏ Keep your car keys separate from your house keys.

❏ Keep the title to the vehicle in a safe place at home, not in the car. Also keep your vehicle registration, mail or bills that list your home address separate from your car. (But you need to keep a photocopy of the registration handy in your wallet in case a police officer stops you.)

❏ Don't tag your key ring with your name and address. If the key chain is lost or stolen, that can lead the thief to your car and home.

❏ Avoid leaving your car unattended in public parking lots for long periods. Park in well-lighted areas with busy pedestrian traffic, if possible.

❏ When you park, turn your wheels sharply into the curb to make it harder to push or tow.

❏ Etch the vehicle identification number in several spots on your car. Check with local police; some departments offer this as a free service.

❏ When buying a car, look for manufacturers' anti-theft options, such as an alarm system, interior hood and trunk releases and a locking steering column. You can also have an alarm installed afterward by a store that specializes in auto electronics.

❏ If you have an alarm, get a sticker announcing that fact and put it where it can be seen.

❏ Even if you don't have a car alarm, get an alarm sticker for the window.

❏ Don't tempt thieves by leaving valuables visible in your car.

Anti-Theft Hardware for Your Car

Auto theft is so rampant today that insurance companies often give you discounts on your policy if you install an anti-theft device. Check with your insurer.

However, no device makes your vehicle completely theft-proof, says Steve Cindrich, senior manager with the National Insurance Crime Bureau. You still should use common sense about parking your car in places where the thief won't have the cover of darkness or the isolation that will give him time to defeat your anti-theft device.

Some gadgets and methods intended to foil car thieves include the following:

VIN etching. Acid-etching the vehicle identification number (VIN) of your car into all windows makes the car easier for police to identify and less attractive to thieves. A thief has to replace all the glass before he can sell the vehicle, police say. Ask if your local police department offers this service. (See advice under "Tips For Avoiding Auto Theft" in this chapter.)

Community registration. Check to see if your community offers voluntary programs in which car owners sign a release allowing police to stop their cars between 1 and 5 A.M. to check ownership. Car owners put an identification sticker on the rear window.

Auto alarms. Car alarms can be installed by specialized repair shops, or by the manufacturer of a new car. The *Consumer Reports* annual buying guide reviews features and gives buying advice.

Safety film on the windows. Some window tinting shops for autos can install safety film that makes it harder to break the glass.

Steering-wheel locking devices. The Club and other devices available at discount stores and auto-parts shops deter thieves. The devices immobilize the steering wheel so that the car cannot be steered.

Theft-deterrent collar. The collar prevents thieves from cracking the steering column and bypassing the ignition. These may be available from some police departments and civic groups; however, they are primarily used for certain older General Motors cars that had the "Saginaw steering column," which has since been redesigned.

LoJack and Teletrac. These brand-name vehicle recovery systems use a transmitter to lead police to a stolen car. A homing device is installed in a secret location on the car. When the owner notifies police that the car has been stolen, the police activate equipment that tracks the auto. The National Insurance Crime Bureau says the devices won't pre-

What to Do if Your Car Is Stolen:

☛ Call police immediately.

☛ Know your location exactly.

☛ Have ready your license tag number, model name and year and other identifying information.

☛ Call your insurer.

Where Most Cars Are Stolen

States with the highest theft rate per 100,000 population:
1. California (1,037.1)
2. New York (932.3)
3. Florida (828)
4. Texas (821.7)
5. Arizona (821.5)

vent theft of a car, but they help insurers and police recover it quickly.

Engine kill switch. This cuts off the fuel supply if a thief is able to start the car and drive off. These devices are available in auto supply stores.

Watch for police department auto theft crime prevention fairs, where you can learn more about car security hardware.

Profile of a Car Thief

Many autos are stolen by thrill-seeking kids or robbers in search of getaway cars. Snatched from driveways, shopping malls, movie theater and condo parking lots, these ordinary Camaros, Cutlasses and Firebirds are often abandoned or sold for parts. But the profile of the ordinary car thief doesn't fit Jose C. Fuentes, who specializes in expensive autos favored by rich professionals. "I'm doing the upper end, not stealing somebody's Camaro who has to work for a living," says Fuentes, of Miami.

Fuentes never met a Porsche he couldn't steal. His tactics: at fancy restaurants, he hands valet attendants fake ticket stubs and walks away with the keys. He prowls hospital parking lots in doctors' whites and a stethoscope. He stalks the parking lots of law firms, hunting for targets. Even if he doesn't have a key, he's so skilled that you can count to 20 and he's gone—with your 911 Carrera.

He and his pals use sophisticated gadgets, such as police scanners and radar-frequency detectors, so they can tell if police are on their trail. "If somebody comes, we just leave," he says.

Police never catch him in the act. They usually trip him up when he goes to sell the hot parts and somebody tips them off. "It's more like a cat-and-mouse game," he says. "They do their job and I do mine."

Protecting Yourself from Carjackers

For most of us, the car has always been a safety zone. But that all changed in the early 1990s, when robbers began commandeering cars at gunpoint. "This is incredibly anxiety-producing because the car is a very private and highly personalized space," says Raymond Norvaco, a professor at the University of California–Irvine.

Carjackings occur in good neighborhoods as well as bad. Robbers approach drivers as they wait at red lights, as they get into their cars in shopping centers, or as they buy gas. Ordered to turn over their keys and get out, drivers have been shot and killed if they don't move fast enough.

"It's really a crime of opportunity," says FBI Special Agent Bob Pocia, of Philadelphia. "It's anybody, everybody, anywhere, anytime. Anybody is a potential victim. . . . Men are just as likely to be carjacked."

The type of auto is also irrelevant. Carjackers have stolen both expensive cars and junkers. Often, the autos are found within hours abandoned on a street, as if the robber simply needed a ride.

In 1992, Congress made carjacking a federal crime with a prison sentence of up to 15 years, depending on the degree of violence.

Tips against Carjacking

Here are some tips from Charlotte, N.C., crime prevention expert David Sells, the FBI and others on how to avoid becoming a victim of carjacking:

❑ Be alert. Watch for people loitering and watching your auto or other vehicles. If anyone pays specific interest to you, attempt to make eye contact. An attacker is less likely to choose a victim who appears prepared and confident.

❏ Know the area you drive. Check your normal routes of travel for potential hazardous conditions. Don't overlook the garage and driveway—carjackings have occurred there, too.

❏ Drive in the center lane so you can't be approached from the curb. Note the routine flow of traffic. Which lane provides you greatest mobility? What are other available avenues of escape?

❏ Anticipate situations. How do you expect the confrontation to occur in each site? As you predict the nature of the assault, plan a response to each site.

❏ Keep your vehicle moving whenever possible. At stoplights, leave room between you and the vehicle in front so you don't get hemmed in by a two-car team of carjackers. Adjust your driving speed so that you won't get stopped at lights.

For more information, contact:

The National Insurance Crime Bureau, 10330 S. Roberts Road, Palos Hills, IL 60465. 708-430-2430; 800-447-6282.

The National Crime Prevention Council, 1700 K Street NW, Second Floor, Washington, D.C. 20006-3817. Phone: 202-466-6272.

The National Safety Council. Central region: 800-621-7619; Western Region, 800-848-5588; Northeastern Region, 800-432-5251; Southeastern Region, 800-441-5103.

If you have information about an auto theft ring or other organized crime activity to defraud an insurer, call 1-800-TEL-NICB. Rewards of up to $1,000 may be paid for information leading to successful prosecution.

❏ If you feel threatened at a stoplight, look both ways and keep going. Police say it's not legal to run a red light, but in practice, they may hesitate to enforce the law under these circumstances. "If it's safe to go through, go through. . . . The safety of the public is our first priority," says Philadelphia Police Capt. David Testa.

❏ Sound your car horn repeatedly. If the car is equipped with an alarm, press that button. The noise will draw attention to you, confuse your attacker and warn others that you are moving.

❏ Beware of bump-and-rob artists. If your car is hit from behind, stay in the car, signal the other driver to follow and go to the nearest police or fire station, gas station or shopping mall. Don't pull over by the side of the road, where you can be robbed.

❏ If you are involved in a minor accident, stay in your car and wait for the police to arrive before you get out. Sometimes a carjacker will bump your car from behind. If you leave your car, a second carjacker will enter it and drive off. Exit your vehicle only if your safety is not compromised.

❏ Look for safe havens along your routes. A safe haven can be a police station, hospital, fire department or even a friend's house. It's any safe location where you can get help.

❏ Keep on main thoroughfares, especially after dark and in high-crime areas.

❏ Keep your car in good condition and the gas tank full.

❏ Keep your doors locked and windows closed. On a hot day, run the air conditioner, or if you don't have one, crank your windows down just enough for ventilation, but not enough for someone to reach into the car.

❏ Be vigilant in parking lots. Select well-lighted spots

near your destination. When returning, have your keys ready in your hand.

❏ If a car follows you to your driveway at night, stay in your car with the doors locked. Don't get out until you can determine the person has a legitimate purpose. If necessary, sound your horn to alert your neighbors.

❏ If confronted by a carjacker, give up your vehicle, but try to get a good look at the suspect so you can describe him to police. Fighting back is a poor choice. Says Akron, Ohio, Police Detective Pete Vidican: "What's worth more? Your car or your life?"

❏ Make sure you have memorized in advance the license plate number of your car. The sooner police have all the necessary information on the suspect and the missing vehicle, the faster they can move on your case.

7

Weapons and Self-Defense Devices

Fed up with crime, some Americans are turning to self-defense devices to protect themselves. But making the decision to carry such a device—whether it's a non-lethal dye that marks an assailant for later identification, or something as controversial and dangerous as a handgun—is not easy. If you choose to acquire a self-protection device, be aware that you must be trained in its use and physically and emotionally able to use it to distract or incapacitate the attacker on the very first try so that you and others around you can survive the confrontation.

Even the mildest of self-defense gadgets carries drawbacks and dangers. Tear gas, for example, can go off in your pocket accidentally. A device that is out of reach is useless. Some experts cite cases in which chemical sprays failed or had the opposite effect—they actually enraged the attacker and made the outcome worse for the victim. And then there's another problem: "Anything that can be taken away by a perpetrator and used against the victim is not a good idea," says Miami Police spokesman Angelo Bitsis.

Jaye Shapiro, a Detroit expert in women's self-defense, worries that self-defense devices make people overconfident. "Use them in combination with other strategies," she says. That means attempting to escape first. It also means learning how to use a chemical spray, but also knowing how to defend the canister with your free hand. Beginning with the least lethal, here are some devices commonly sold for self-defense:

Dyes. An aerosol can sprays a seven-foot pressurized stream of dye that congeals into foam. Manufacturers claim the product can't be washed off for days, enabling you or the police to identify the assailant later. One manufacturer makes a locking wallet that sprays a thief with blue dye if it is forced open.

Siren alarms. Personal shriek alarms, often worn around the wrist or neck, send out a piercing 130-decibel wail when activated, ostensibly drawing attention. Some experts question the effectiveness of siren alarms because people may ignore them and not come to your aid. One advantage: they can't be used against you.

Chemical defense sprays. One form is a type of tear gas, such as the brand-name Mace, which causes an intense burning sensation. Another is a spray based on the active ingredients in hot peppers. Pepper spray inflames the eyes of the attacker, causing temporary blindness. Some sprays combine both features. The sprays, which usually cost less than $30 and are sold at some gun and discount stores, can be sprayed from a distance of about 15 feet.

Some concerns: chemical sprays sold to the public may be inferior in quality to those marketed to police. Once purchased, people rarely test them to see if they are effective. Also, most people can't get these items into their hands quickly enough when they need them.

Hand-held stun guns. Stun guns zap an attacker with electricity. One version uses 70,000 volts, but to be effective, the two electrodes on the end of the gun must make contact with the attacker. Heavy clothing may lessen their effectiveness, too. They can be a danger to innocent people around you. Stun guns and other electric devices are prohibited in some states. Check with your local police department.

Self-Defense Devices

Buyers should keep these tips in mind:

☛ A can of pepper spray in your purse is no guarantee you'll be able to ward off an attacker. Neither is a hand-held siren. People routinely ignore alarms, especially in high-crime areas. Pepper spray and tear gas sprays can become inert in their canisters, or may be of inferior quality.

☛ Control your weapon. Stun guns, tear-gas sprays and other deterrents can be snatched away by an assailant and used on you. Practice using the devices so you can react instantly in an emergency.

☛ Don't break the law. Some states ban many self-defense products, such as electric stun guns, metallic knuckles and other weapons. Call your local police department to find out what's legal in your area before purchasing a self-defense device.

Dogs

Dogs are a time-honored self-defense device. They can protect you while walking, jogging or bicycling, and they are excellent security guards at home.

Dog trainers say some of the best guard dogs are German shepherds, Doberman pinschers and Rottweilers. They're natural protectors, territorial, fiercely loyal and fairly easy to train for protection. If you want a dog that does more barking than biting, consider cocker spaniels, golden retrievers and Labradors.

Noise is a great deterrent. A barking dog attracts attention—and the last thing a burglar wants is attention.

Your dog needn't be an attack dog, says Joe Mele, assistant professor of the National Crime Prevention Institute in Louisville, Ky. "A very territorial dog that barks when someone comes near your property can create a tremendous amount of noise," Mele says. "Sometimes a small dog that won't stop barking can be as effective as a larger dog." Research in England showed little fox terriers to be the best watchdogs of all: "They don't shut up," Mele says.

To be trainable, a dog must have a strong personality, it must be attentive, and it must react to situations. An indifferent or lazy dog is not good for protection purposes.

Trainers recommend getting a dog as a puppy so that your relationship begins early.

Remember that a trained dog can be a deadly weapon. All dogs have the potential to bite, harming their owners, neighbors—or criminals. You're responsible for keeping it away from people who mean no harm.

For this reason, take into account the kind of neighborhood you live in. Are there a lot of children around who may tease the dog? A teased dog is unhappy—sometimes unhappy enough to bite.

Post a "Beware of the Dog" sign on your property for the final touch, even if you don't have a dog.

Guns

Nationwide, more than 200 million guns are in the possession of private citizens, according to the U.S. Bureau of

Alcohol, Tobacco and Firearms. A handgun is present in one in four U.S. households.

Every year, more than 24,000 Americans are killed with handguns through homicide, suicide and accident. In 1990, 1,416 people were accidentally killed with firearms.

Police officers say the last thing they need on the streets are more guns, but they also walk a fine line on the issue. "People have a right to defend themselves," says Angelo Bitsis, a spokesman for the Miami Police Department. "But at the same time, the more guns out there, the more chance there is for something to go wrong. The gun can be stolen and used in another crime. It can be used against the owner. We don't want people taking the law into their own hands and yet they have a right to defend themselves. It's a tough decision, like a lot of things these days."

Are guns effective for personal defense? Some studies suggest they are, others that they are not.

The one point of universal agreement in this issue is that anyone buying a gun inherits enormous responsibility and potential liability.

All prospective purchasers must confront these issues: Can you handle and store a gun safely, particularly if you have children at home? Will you learn how to carry and use it legally? Can you envision yourself shooting someone with it?

This last point is particularly important. "If you're going to buy a gun for defense, the threshold you have to get past is not, 'Well, I want a gun, but I would never shoot anybody.' It doesn't work that way," says Andrew Kallergis, who runs a gun store and range in Pompano Beach, Fla. "A gun is not a scaring device. It's not the magic wand. Most criminals are not afraid of guns.

"You have to have the mental attitude that you're going

Protection Tips: Without a Gun

You're not prepared to fire a gun at another human being, even one who presents a significant threat. Many options exist for people who decide not to arm themselves but want to improve their chances of avoiding or minimizing violent crime.

Here is a review of some of the most important and obvious ways. These recommendations come from veteran police officers Walter Philbrick and Shawnee Fross, who also are officials of International Protective Services Inc., a Hollywood, Fla., firm specializing in crime prevention, gun safety and security.

☛ On the street, be aware of your surroundings. Before leaving your car or a building, look for people and occupied vehicles in or near your path. Be especially aware of vans, increasingly favored by criminals. Always have an escape route in mind. Keep jewelry and watches covered by clothing until you are safely at your destination.

☛ Don't behave like a potential victim. Appear confident and assertive. At the same time, don't call attention to yourself. Blend into your surroundings; don't stand out in a crowd. Always trust your instincts. If you sense something is wrong, take immediate evasive action. Apologize later if you guessed wrong.

☛ Consider an intermediate weapon such as pepper spray, a baton or umbrella. Be sure it is immediately accessible and be prepared and trained to use it. A mere show of force could get you hurt or killed.

☛ If attacked, consider creating a diversion. Scream, fall down, fake a heart attack, anything the criminal does not expect. In any case, get enough information to provide a good description of your assailant. Look for scars, tattoos, a beard, a mustache, or an accent to help police track down your attacker.

☛ In a purse snatching, let go of the purse and gently fall to the ground. This minimizes the chances of being knocked down. (Some experts advise throwing the purse in one direction and running in the other.) Do not fight merely to protect your possessions. They're not worth it.

☞ Plan ahead. Store packages and other valuables in the trunk of your car before you leave home, not when you arrive at a destination. Keep money, credit cards and expensive rings in your pocket. If confronted, turn over your purse or wallet.

☞ When stopping at traffic lights, keep at least one-half car length between you and the vehicle in front, providing room to maneuver away from trouble. Tint your windows as dark as legally acceptable; at night, someone outside can't tell who is inside.

☞ Keep your vehicle well-maintained. Frequently check your tires, battery and fan belts. A crippled vehicle could leave you in peril. Buy a portable cellular phone and keep it on. Keep someone aware of your location and expected time of arrival.

☞ Consider a burglar alarm and other security measures for your home. Go outside at night and study your home from all four corners. See what a potential intruder may see and take corrective action.

☞ Have a "safe room" at home, one equipped with a solid door and a phone. A cellular phone is best, because burglars sometimes cut regular phone lines. If threatened, retreat to the room, call police and do not leave until police have secured the house.

to do what you have to do to protect yourself, because otherwise you'll end up getting yourself killed."

Discuss the issue with members of your family. Remember that gun registration and training are essential if you decide to purchase a gun, as is finding a safe location for the gun in your home or office.

Consult your local police department about the pros and cons of gun ownership for crime protection. Find out what local gun laws apply to you. Gun laws vary from state to state, and even from city to city. Call your local police department to ask what laws apply in your area. Criminal background checks are required before a gun can be sold to you. Some states have waiting periods; others require licenses to carry a concealed weapon. Your home state may also require training and certification.

Ask your police department under what conditions the use of deadly force is questionable or open to interpretation.

If you decide not to purchase a gun, consider other self-protection measures and/or training.

Gun Safety Rules for Parents

❑ Begin teaching children gun safety as soon as a child starts acting out "gun play" or asking about guns. Teach children to follow these four steps if they find a gun: 1. Stop. 2. Don't touch. 3. Leave the area. 4. Tell an adult.

❑ Ask if guns are present at homes where your child plays. If so, and you let your child play there, make sure gun safety rules are followed.

❑ If you have a gun at home, lock it in a secure place where children can't reach it.

❑ Lock ammunition in a different, secure place.

❑ Keep the gun unloaded in case children accidentally come across it.

8

Crime-Proofing Your Money

It's not enough to say: I'm too smart to be ripped off. I'll never fall victim to a con artist or let my credit cards be pilfered. Remember that while the rest of us are busy taking the kids to school, working, grabbing dinner and mowing the lawn, con artists are busy developing subtle, sometimes high-tech swindles.

Take this early-morning call in Detroit. "I'm sorry to wake you," said the caller, "but this is your niece, and I'm in trouble."

"Donna?" mumbled the awakened party.

"Yes, this is Donna," the caller said, and then poured out a tangled story of desperation. She had been picked up for speeding and the police found a gun, which was, of course, carried only for protection. Now she was in jail and needed $300 cash bond to get out. It was just a loan; she would pay it back tomorrow. Her best friend lived a few blocks away and could be by in five minutes to pick it up.

The aunt bailed out her niece, but learned soon afterward

that the real Donna had been sound asleep in her own bed all night. She has been scammed by a stranger. "It can happen to anyone. I know," contends Esther Shapiro, head of Detroit's Consumer Affairs Department. "It happened to me."

If experts can get taken, the rest of us need to watch out. Despite attempts to keep the public on alert, thousands of people every day respond to telephone marketing scams, reciting their credit card and bank account numbers to criminal con artists.

Scams are big business. Telemarketing and mail fraud cost us $10 billion to $40 billion a year. Insurance, investment and credit frauds also are in the multibillion-dollar range, and the list goes on: Quickie diets, sweepstakes and travel bargains continue to bilk consumers at every age and income level.

To get an idea of how quickly a scam can surface, consider what happened after the FBI arrested more than 200 people nationwide during a telemarketing fraud sting in 1993. Other swindlers immediately began calling victims of the apprehended con artists. The callers offered help in getting the victims' money back from an FBI "recovered money pool." The hitch: they had to pay an advance fee of up to thousands of dollars. "In the hands of a con artist, a telephone is a dangerous assault weapon," says Hubert H. Humphrey III, Minnesota attorney general and president of the National Association of Attorneys General.

This is where you come in. Learn the common ruses used by thieves and how to combat them. There are countless scams. Below are some of the most popular ones. All scams have a common theme: they prey on people who want something for nothing (so keep your greed in check), or people who don't keep alert.

Credit Card Schemes

Plastic is convenient—for you and for thieves. As we shall see, a thief can ring up thousands of dollars in charges in your name without even touching your cards. The cost of credit card fraud is immense: more than $1 billion worldwide for MasterCard and Visa in 1991, according to Alex Hart, president of MasterCard International.

With more than 600 million credit cards in circulation worldwide, credit card fraud has hit record levels. "It's out of control," says Suzanne Lynch, president of the Michigan chapter of the International Association of Credit Card Investigators. About half the fraud is related to lost or stolen cards, but you may be surprised to hear about other credit card scams.

Theft without even stealing your cards. Two credit card crooks in Detroit had their victim's Social Security number, birth date and home address. With that, they got a fake ID in his name from the Secretary of State's office. Next, they applied for instant lines of credit—and soon were on a $20,000 spending spree. "I was dumbfounded at how easy it was to access a person's credit without having solid identification," says victim Charlie Williams. "I really felt invaded."

Intercepted cards. Thieves like to get their hands on your credit card before it even reaches you through the mail. Some companies now are sending cards by express overnight delivery to make sure cards aren't intercepted. Thieves steal from mail trucks or mailboxes. Postal workers toiling in the back rooms of post offices have been caught on government cameras diverting carts of credit cards from the mail stream. Interception of any type results in the majority of MasterCard's fraud cases in the United States, says Philip Verdi, a company executive vice president.

Recoding magnetic strips. Crooks now know how to recode the magnetic strips found on the backs of credit cards, which means the information won't match the name and number embossed on the front of the card. How the scam works: a restaurant employee takes your credit card to a back room and runs it through a machine (some of whose components are available at ordinary electronics stores). The machine transfers the code from your card to another card—and the thief goes on a spending spree. Also, a special computer accessory is now available that allows thieves to recode magnetic strips with credit card numbers obtained from tossed-out receipts. Another ploy is to re-emboss credit cards with a fake number.

Lost and stolen cards. Thieves use lost or stolen credit cards to buy all sorts of things. Sometimes they order expensive merchandise for delivery to vacant homes. They ask that the goods be left outside or in a porch or garage, says Raymond Walsh, assistant Wayne County prosecutor in Detroit.

Protection from Credit Card Fraud

The good news is that most credit card companies will limit your financial liability for bogus charges as long as you report your stolen cards immediately. The bad news is that the losses often are passed on to customers in the form of higher interest rates, annual fees or store prices. So you still pay in the end.

You can help keep costs down and thieves at a distance by employing these strategies every time you pull out your credit card:

Carry only the credit cards and blank checks you need

How thieves use credit cards

Some of the ways enterprising thieves can rob you blind using your credit cards:

536 244 777 4?

21 42 45 333 677 2

22 45 355 200

3688 3098 2093

WHY YOU SHOULD CARE: Credit card fraud cost more than $1 billion worldwide for MasterCard and Visa in 1991.

Credit card scams

Intercepting cards
Thieves take your cards before you get them, stealing from mail trucks or mailboxes. This is the most common type of credit card fraud in the U.S.

Getting credit with fake ID
Thieves get your Social Security number, birthdate and home address; with that, they get fake ID and lines of instant credit in your name; then they go on a shopping spree.

Recoding magnetic strips
Using a jerry-rigged recoder, thieves transfer the code from your card to another card or they use a special computer accessory to recode magnetic strips with credit card numbers from tossed-out receipts. All the charges on the altered cards are then billed to you.

Lost or stolen cards
Thieves use lost or stolen cards to buy whatever they want, often ordering merchandise over the phone for delivery to vacant houses.

SOURCES: Federal Bureau of Investigation 1992 Uniform Crime Reports, Master Card International, International Association of Credit Card Investigators

immediately, in case of theft or loss. If you're not using charge cards, lock them up at home, says Raymond Walsh, assistant Wayne County prosecutor in Detroit.

Get your charge card back immediately after using it. Don't leave it sitting on sales counters, on hotel registration desks or on restaurant tables. The account number can be quickly copied or memorized, even if no one touches the card.

Always take your receipts and carbons. This prevents someone from telephoning in catalog orders or making other purchases charged to the account numbers read on the receipts. A few restaurant servers have been caught doctoring tip amounts on charge slips, so your receipt could come in doubly handy. If you're paying by check, never let a merchant copy your credit card number as proof of identification, or else he may be tempted to ring up charges on the card. A merchant can, however, note the type of card and expiration date.

Other tips:

❏ Sign your cards. Often, retailers check only to see that the signature on the card matches the signature on the sales slip, checking no other ID. "If you don't do it, someone else can just sign your card," says Mary Beth Butler of the consumer group Bankcard Holders of America.

❏ Get a credit card with your picture on it. A merchant will know the card belongs to you, not an impostor.

❏ Hold no more than four or five cards. "Cut them down to an essential few," says Shapiro, of Detroit's consumer affairs. A universal card is good almost anywhere.

❏ Cut up credit card bills if you throw them away. Don't leave them intact; thieves sometimes rummage through trash to find credit card numbers. Cut up cards you no longer use. Obliterate the account numbers so thieves can't read the numbers.

❏ Consider traveler's checks when going out of town. American Express introduced traveler's checks with the amount of the check printed on the back: The number on the left side smears to the touch, while the number on the right side does not. This type of printing is very difficult for counterfeiters to reproduce.

❏ Memorize the personal identification numbers (PINs) you use at automatic teller machines. Do not write down your PINs, or a thief may make use of them.

❏ Carefully read monthly statements to make sure all charges are yours. If any seem suspicious, call your credit card company. Call if you don't get a monthly bill on time. Someone may have dipped into your mailbox to steal your bill—and the account number.

❏ Don't give your account number to anyone who calls you on the phone. If you want to buy something, call the company back.

❏ Make sure that the card you get back from a restaurant or business is your own. Unscrupulous clerks may switch your card with a look-alike card that already has been spent to the limit.

❏ If a caller claims to represent a credit card company and asks for your account number, don't oblige. Obviously, credit card companies already know your number. Crooks don't.

What to Do if You're a Victim

Report lost or stolen cards right away. Call your credit card companies; their names and phone numbers and your account numbers should be kept on a list at home in case of theft. Also consider calling the police.

How to foil credit card thieves

Some tips for keeping thieves at bay whenever you use your credit card:

Carry only the credit cards and blank checks you need

Consider keeping credit cards in a locked safe at home when you're not using them.

Get your charge card back immediately after using it

Don't leave your card sitting on sales counters, registration desks or restaurant tables, where the account number could be copied or memorized.

Get receipts and carbons

This prevents thieves from using your card number to make purchases.

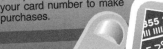

Don't let merchants copy your credit card number

If merchants require a credit card as identification when you pay by check, let them note only the type of card and expiration date.

If your card is lost or stolen...

Call the credit card company right away; if the card was stolen, call the police.

SOURCES: Federal Bureau of Investigation 1992 Uniform Crime Reports, Master Card International, International Association of Credit Card Investigators

Memorize personal identification numbers (PINs) you use at ATMs

Don't tuck them in your wallet where thieves could find them.

Don't give your card number to anyone who calls on the phone

Call the company back if you want to buy something.

Sweepstakes Scams

You can't be a winner in a contest you didn't enter. No one is waiting around for you to phone and claim expensive prizes, regardless of the promotional pitch.

Yet hope springs eternal. Innocents believe that it is illegal for a lie to be carried on a postcard. Some sweepstakes ask you to claim your prize by calling a 900 number—only to leave you footing a phone charge of $4.98 a minute or so.

Dealing with sweepstakes fraud is a lot like peeling an onion. No sooner is one layer removed than a different one is revealed, with its own special character. Twenty years ago, it was a simple scam: you got a postcard saying you had won a trip to Hawaii, you sent off a $25 check. That was it. No trip. No refund. No way to catch the promoter.

Then the promised prizes became bigger—as much as $500,000. The person on the other end of the phone line insisted it was not really a sweepstakes, but marketing research. The prize was offered in return for the purchase and evaluation of $500 in vitamins or cosmetics or cleaning products. Lots of people bought the products. No one got the prize.

The introduction of the 900 area code for telephone lines adds a new dimension to sweepstakes scams. The victim calls the number to claim a prize and waits as long as 20 minutes as the identifying code number on the postcard or legal-looking document is checked against the "prize list"— ringing up a big phone bill.

Today, you have to avoid not only sweepstakes, but "sweepstakes prize finders."

"We know you are eligible for a $100,000 award," says the pitch. "We can get it for you—for a finder's fee." A widow in Michigan was promised her long-awaited prize in return for a $4,000 advance payment. She wasn't aware her name had been added to a list circulated by a well-organized criminal network. Having determined she was successfully duped in the past, the so-called recovery specialists stepped in to drain whatever cash might be left.

Ripped Off?

Don't turn red and humbly accept that you've been scammed. Report it and help put bogus companies out of business. Contact your local Better Business Bureau, state attorney general's office and local consumer protection agency.

How to Avoid Being Conned

You can avoid being duped. Many legitimate companies conduct contests with expensive prizes as part of their promotional program. If you are in doubt, contact the company directly. The Federal Trade Commission also has this advice:

❏ Watch out if your winning announcement carries any payment conditions, such as prepaid taxes, refundable deposits or shipping costs. If the prize is real, the promoter will pay the delivery charge and taxes will be withheld or the winnings reported to the IRS. You will not be asked to pay taxes up front.

❏ If you think you've won the big one, check it out by calling the legitimate major sweepstakes outfits toll-free. Reach Publisher's Clearinghouse at 800-645-9242; American Family Publishers at 800-237-2400; Million Dollar Dream

Sweepstakes (Time Inc.) at 800-541-1000; and Reader's Digest Sweepstakes at 800-234-9000.

❏ Realize that some time-share resorts offer prizes or vacations to lure naive consumers to high-pressure sales presentations.

❏ Think carefully before sending a check to contest promotion companies. If you're asked to use delivery systems other than the post office, the company may be trying to avoid detection and prosecution by postal inspectors.

❏ Don't be fooled. If it sounds too good to be true, it is.

For More Information

If you think you've been scammed, contact the nonprofit Alliance for Fraud in Telemarketing, c/o National Consumers League, 815 15th St. NW, Suite 928N, Washington, D.C. 20005. Call 800-876-7060.

Also, contact the U.S. Postal Inspection Service if you suspect mail fraud. Your local post office will have a phone number for inspectors.

If You've Been Scammed

If you've been scammed, assume your name is on a sucker list, according to the Washington, D.C.,-based organization Call For Action. You can expect offers from more flimflam artists working telephones nationwide. Be doubly cautious next time.

Telephone Credit Cards

You're making a call from an airport or shopping mall. Little do you realize that someone is watching over your shoulder as you recite or punch in your 14-digit long-distance card authorization code. The thief may be dressed as a salesperson and pretend to be doing business at an adjacent phone. Soon, the cheater is gone—selling your access code on the street moments later. The seller may feed your numbers by beeper to waiting accomplices at separate phone banks, where calls to anywhere in the world are sold for $10 or $20 each, says Peggy Snyder, executive director of the Communication Fraud Control Association.

The snooping-over-the-shoulder trend is called "shoulder surfing," and telecommunications fraud is estimated to bring more than $2 billion in losses a year.

Some surfers use binoculars to snatch numbers. Others use camcorders, looking for all the world like someone waiting to videotape Uncle Stanley getting off the plane at the airport. The underground network behind the illicit calls ranges from high-tech hackers who break into business phone systems via computer to street-corner hustlers selling stolen calling-card numbers.

Long-distance carriers have established round-the-clock monitoring operations to fight back. These operations compare card activity to your normal usage patterns. Phone companies may call you immediately when fraud is suspected. A compromised card can be deactivated within an hour.

Avoiding Telephone Fraud

Long-distance companies offer the following suggestions on what you can do to avoid telephone fraud:

❏ Use magnetic-line-reading "card swipe" phones whenever possible. That way, your card won't be sitting face up in a readable position for several minutes while you punch in a code.

❑ Block the view of the telephone key pad as you punch in your access code.

❑ Speak softly when reciting your access code.

Bell Atlantic has started offering customers a calling card imprinted with only 10 digits. The customer can choose—and memorize—the remaining four digits of the code to thwart snooping thieves.

If you are victimized by thieves, tell your phone company. Remember that when calls are billed to your credit card, long-distance carriers—not you—often eat most or all of the losses.

How to Spot Phone Service Scams

☛ A stranger calls and asks you to help with a phone company investigation. All you have to do is say "Yes" to the operator for a bunch of international calls that will be billed to a third party. You're told you won't be billed—but you are.

☛ You open a long-distance phone bill from a company whose service you never joined. The scam: A telemarketer tried to change your carrier without your consent.

Government Scams

In Wisconsin, a private organization listed its 800 number in local telephone books right next to the 800 number listing for Medicare and Social Security information. When people called the wrong 800 number, they heard a recording instructing them to call a toll-bearing 900 number. They were billed for information they could have received free.

Is there a new baby in the family? Mom and Dad will get an official-looking missive offering to get the infant a Social Security number for a fee. You can do it yourself for free. Call the Social Security Administration at 800-772-1213, or check your local phone book for the office near you.

Newly married or divorced women may want a change of name; they get the same offer. Few people realize that birth, marriage and divorce records are public; anyone checking them can compile a profitable mailing list.

Magazine and radio ads peddle books listing federal auctions and special information about government programs at prices as high as $75. It's all free government stuff. Call 800-555-1212 to ask the operator for the toll-free number for the government agency you need.

Employment Swindles

One popular employment swindle involves the sale of job lists. Someone out of work pays $50 or $100 for a list of "guaranteed" job openings that turns out to have been typed from the newspaper classified ads. Another is a phone scam: call a 900 number to learn about jobs paying $50 to $60 an hour in, let's say, Kuwait. An unwitting caller may not realize that phone charges piled up by the minute.

More than 175 scams have opened and closed in Florida alone in two years, says Stuart Rado, executive director of National Consumer Fraud Task Force in Miami Beach. The typical scam: A newspaper ad says construction workers can earn $70,000 tax free. Callers find out they must pay $298 in advance as a security deposit to cover the cost of faxes, phone calls and other overhead charges in case you back out of any job offer. Callers are told to write "fully refundable security deposit" on the memo line of their checks, and an overnight delivery service will show up to pick up the check. They're assured that if no job is offered within six months, they get their money back. But six months later, the phone is disconnected.

Loan Scams

You read an ad that promises a loan as long you pay a fee in advance. Often, it asks you to dial a toll-free number or, at times, a 900 number that brings a hefty charge on your next phone bill. That charge still is smaller than the advance loan fee. That fee is usually $100 to several hundred dollars. It may seem worth it for a struggling company or family, except for what happens next: the money is sent in, and the loan company is never heard from again. No loan.

The Federal Trade Commission is investigating complaints about financially strapped customers and small business owners getting duped by companies guaranteeing loans. Don't confuse these schemes with legitimate loan sources. Banks, for instance, will charge you a fee to process a loan—but they may not guarantee you'll get a loan or say that your advance fee will be credited toward repaying your loan.

To protect yourself:

❑ Be wary of ads saying that bad credit is no problem in getting a loan. If you can't get a loan from a legitimate bank, then you aren't likely to get one by reading a classified ad.

❑ Be leery of unfamiliar lenders with toll-free and 900 numbers.

❑ Check out the company with a local consumer protection agency and the state Attorney General's Office to see if they've received complaints. Questionable companies, though, often milk an area for a few months, collect their loan fees, then skip town to set up shop in another state before complaints pour in. So if your consumer offices don't have records of complaints, it still doesn't mean an advance-fee loan business is legitimate.

❏ Ask to have any company's offer in writing. Make sure you understand a contract before signing.

If you have been scammed by a loan operation, contact your local consumer protection agency, the Better Business Bureau, the state attorney general's office, the FTC suggests. Or contact Call for Action, an international nonprofit network of consumer hotlines, at 202-537-0585. You also can file a complaint with the FTC. Write: FTC, Division of Credit Practices, Washington, D.C. 20580.

If you are desperate because you have bad credit, contact the nonprofit Consumer Credit Counseling Service to arrange repayment plans to pay off your debts. Check your telephone directory to find the office near you or send a self-addressed, stamped envelope to: National Foundation for Consumer Credit, 8611 Second Ave., Suite 100, Silver Spring, Md. 20910. Call 800-388-2227.

Always check out a company before doing business. Consider driving to its office instead of calling. You are your wallet's best protector—not the salesman.

Home-Improvement Scams

Actor Richard Dreyfuss depicted the quintessential aluminum-siding con artist in the movie *Tin Men*: He's a shady salesman who shows up on a doorstep saying he has materials left over from a job in your neighborhood, so he'll offer you a cheap rate. Or, in the case of the movie, he asks to use your home as a "before" shot in a magazine spread on "before" and "after" remodeling jobs. If you bite, what you may end up with is a shoddy job whose price inflates once you give the OK to start work.

Don't fall for this. Stick to contractors you seek out—not those who magically come to you. Check out their backgrounds for customer complaints by contacting the government department that licenses contractors in your area, the Better Business Bureau or local consumer advocates. Don't sign a contract until an expert reads it over.

Bogus Postcards

A package is being held for you, warns the green postcard. Please call this particular 900 number within seven days to arrange delivery. What package? Honey, did you order something?

Thousands of people have called the 900 number. Some received nothing. Others were shipped a tiny fake diamond pendant. All paid a price: From $9.95 to $28 for the call. "It's like being mugged," says Emma Byrne, New Jersey consumer affairs director. "You haven't been hit over the head, but your pocket has been picked just the same."

You can refuse to pay the phone charges; just call your phone company. But some retirees on fixed incomes are afraid that if they don't pay, their phone service will be cut off. So they become victims of the scam. Some government protection is available. A law in New Jersey, for example, requires 900-line companies to warn callers of the cost of the call and give them a chance to hang up.

Telephone Solicitations

It's early evening and you've just settled down at home. Suddenly, the phone rings. "Congratulations," the caller says. "Your name has been picked at random to win a fabulous prize. But I'll need a credit card number for identification."

Is it a hoax? Usually, says Joel Bloom, regional director of the Federal Trade Commission's New York office. Americans lose an estimated $10 billion a year to these and other scams, though most could easily be avoided. About one in three Americans has fallen prey to an illegal phone scam, according to a survey by Consumer Protection Network. Fraud cases seem to multiply when economic times are hard.

A new sweepstakes fraud uses an 800 number that turns your call into a fee-bearing 900 number call. How it works: hundreds of people have received postcards with the "official notification" that the recipient has "definitely been awarded" two prizes such as U.S. Savings Bonds and $10,000 in cash—and they must be claimed immediately. Since the winner need only call a toll-free number, many call. A recording announces that to claim prizes, you can send in a letter or stay on the line for $3.90 a minute. The winners end up with a phone charge of $11.70 to $15.60. If this happens to you, report it to the phone company.

You may be able to stop telemarketing calls to your home. For a monthly fee, some phone companies will place a special listing under your name that states "No Solicitation Calls." Anyone who disregards that warning can be fined. Ask your phone company about this service.

Short of that, the best defense is to use common sense. If a deal sounds too good to be true, why risk it?

Here are some warning signs to alert you that you may have been targeted for a scam:

❏ Sweepstakes that require you to pay an entry fee or other charges before you're eligible to win.

❏ Deals that require you to call a 900 number. These numbers cost money, sometimes as high as $3.90 a minute.

❏ Letters that have an "official" look, as if they came from the federal government.

❏ Job or business ads that promise easy money for little work.

❏ Deals that require you to give a credit card, bank account or Social Security number. (All of these can lead a thief to your money.)

❏ Deals that promise you easy credit, even if you have a bad credit history.

More Anti-Fraud Tips

The National Fraud Information Center offers tips on protecting yourself from telemarketing and mail fraud:

❏ Ask the telephone solicitor for a name and number to call back or to mail you more information. If you're told you must take advantage of the offer "right now" and can't call back, don't buy. Ditto, if the caller won't mail you information.

Five Ways to Spot a Scam:
☛ You're told you must act today.
☛ You must pay a fee to get your "prize."
☛ The caller refuses to send you information by mail.
☛ The company has a name that can be mistaken for a government agency or a well-known company.
☛ The caller asks for your Social Security number, credit card or calling card number.
Source: Call For Action, Washington, D.C.

❏ Never give your credit card or bank account number unless you're familiar with the company.

❏ Never reveal financial information to strangers.

❏ Never send money orders or checks to a post office box or anywhere else unless you're sure of the company.

❏ Never send cash.

❏ Beware of 900 numbers, or shipping and handling fees that exceed the cost of the item you're ordering.

❏ When anyone tells you that you have won a prize, hold on to your money.

❏ Never act on an impulse.

If you suspect a scam, contact consumer protection agencies, better business bureaus or your state attorney general's office.

The federal government has a free booklet that lists more than 2,000 places to call if you've been stung by fraud or a bad consumer deal. To order the *Consumer Resource Handbook*, write to Handbook, Pueblo, Colo. 81009.

Several states have laws dealing with telemarketing fraud, but many lack legislation tailored to the elusive nature of the scams and their cross-state operations, says Karen McFarland, director of Florida's Division of Consumer Services. Florida's law is one of a handful in the nation that currently require licensing. "Truthfully, the real bad guys are not going to get a license," says McFarland. "They'll rent a motel room for a week and then disappear."

For Information

Ask the federal government for a free booklet listing more than 2,000 places to call if you've been stung by fraud or a bad consumer deal. To order the Consumer Resource Handbook, write to: Handbook, Pueblo, Colo. 81009.

Charity Solicitations

If there is one lesson to learn about gifts to nonprofit organizations and protecting yourself from scams, it is this: check out your charity.

Appeals for victims of cancer and heart disease strike a receptive chord in William Connor. Since his bout with throat cancer and his wife's struggles with heart disease and diabetes, he regularly sends small donations to medical charities. "When you go through these things, it kind of hits home," says Connor, a retired Philadelphia office manager. "It makes you think of other people in need."

Among the charities Connor contributed to is one that was sued by Pennsylvania's attorney general for fraudulent fund-raising appeals. State investigators allege that less than 3 percent of donations to the organization is spent on programs directly helping patients. The lesson: Check out an organization before sending money. No matter if the cause is something as worthy as the children of slain police officers, cancer victims or endangered animals.

How to avoid common charity scams:

❏ Evaluate a charity before contributing. Ask for a copy of its annual report, to which you're legally entitled under federal law. Read the financial report to see how much is spent on legitimate programs. Also, some states keep charity tax forms on file.

❏ Contact watchdog groups that monitor fund-raising and spending of national charities. The Better Business Bu-

---

Check out a telemarketing company by writing Call For Action, 3400 Idaho Ave. NW, Washington, D.C. 20016. Or call 202-537-0585.

---

reau's Philanthropic Advisory Service says charities should spend at least 50 percent of donations on helping the needy (or the organization's cause) and fundraising shouldn't exceed 35 percent. The BBB offers a "Give But Give Wisely" list ($2) and an Annual Charity Index ($12.95). Write: 4200 Wilson Blvd., Suite 800, Arlington, Va. 22203; call 703-247-9323.

Another watchdog group, the National Charities Information Bureau, contends at least 60 percent of donations should pay for helping the needy (or the organization's cause). For a free "Wise Giving Guide" and background reports on a prospective national charity, write: NCIB, 19 Union Square West, New York, NY 10003; call 212-929-6300. The first three background reports on individual charities are free.

❏ Beware of look-alike charities. Some have names similar to American Cancer Society, for instance. Donors often are confused by fund-raisers using names similar to those of well-established groups.

❏ Make sure of the group's identity before giving. If a charity claims to be local, find out if it has a local office or spends donations on local programs.

❏ Beware of emotional appeals in the mail, particularly if the charity doesn't give details on how money is spent. Appeals shouldn't be disguised as bills or invoices—that's illegal. Sweepstakes appeals should say you don't have to contribute to be eligible for prizes.

❏ You're under no obligation to pay for unordered merchandise, such as cards and calendars. Don't pay, if you don't want to do so.

❏ In telephone and door-to-door solicitations, don't be pressured into making immediate donations or allow a runner to pick up money. If you're unsure, tell solicitors to mail you information. Don't use credit card numbers over the phone if you don't know the organization.

❑ Find out whether a charity hired a professional fundraising company. That's usually a tip-off that most of your money pays for solicitors—not charity.

The few bad apples only make it harder for legitimate charities to raise money. A 1992 national survey found that the number of people who felt that charities were "honest and ethical in their use of funds" dropped from three-fourths of those surveyed in 1990 to only two-thirds, according to Independent Sector, a New York-based charities support group. The more rigorous that donors become in their giving, the more likely it will be that questionable charities will be run out of business—and legitimate causes will thrive.

Be twice as cautious, but just as generous as always, says Ken Albrecht of the National Charities Information Bureau.

Confidence Games

A man says he found an envelope with money inside, and he's willing to share it with you—as long as you're willing to put up some of your own money as a good-faith gesture. Now, think about that. Why would someone want to give money to you—a total stranger? Why wouldn't he want it all for himself? Some people don't ask themselves those questions, and they get taken. The con artist always manages to make a switch at the last minute. He takes off with your money and leaves you with an envelope stuffed with worthless shredded paper.

Police and newspaper crime reporters have long warned about "pigeon drops," but, still, people are taken by them and other confidence games:

❏ The bank examiner scam. A stranger says he's a bank official and asks for your help in cornering a crooked teller. That is your first clue that this guy is up to no good: Banks never ask citizens to help corner bad employees. The stranger asks you to withdraw money from your bank account and hand it to him. That way, he can check the serial numbers or maybe mark the money to corner the teller. Trouble is, that is the last time you see that money.

❏ Lottery ticket scam. A stranger says he has a big winning lottery ticket but he's an undocumented alien, so he's willing to split the proceeds with you if you'll turn in the ticket for him. First, of course, he'd like you to put up some good-faith cash. And the result is the same as in the pigeon drop: the con artist has left with your money, and all you have is a worthless lottery ticket.

To avoid these scams, avoid the con artists. Don't listen to strangers.

If you fall victim, don't be too embarrassed to report the crimes to police. Con artists will only continue preying on other people as long as their pursuits stay profitable. Your call to police could bring the satisfaction of landing your thief in jail.

Phony Utility Company Scams

Con artists have been known to pose as phone company representatives asking to verify your account number. Realize that the phone company doesn't make such calls. Hang up.

If someone shows up at your door posing as a utility company worker and asks to check out something in your house, ask for identification and call the company to check it out.

Index